INCENTIVE COMPENSATION

and Employee Ownership

THIRD EDITION

INCENTIVE COMPENSATION

and Employee Ownership

THIRD EDITION

Edited by Scott S. Rodrick

The National Center for Employee Ownership
Oakland, California

Incentive Compensation and Employee Ownership
Editing and design by Scott S. Rodrick

The National Center for Employee Ownership
1736 Franklin Street, 8th Floor, Oakland, CA 94612
(510) 208-1300
(510) 272-9510 (fax)
E-mail: *nceo@nceo.org*
Web site: *http://www.nceo.org/*

First edition (under the title *Incentive Compensation for Employee Ownership Companies*) published February 1998

Second edition November 1998

Third edition May 1999; reprinted October 1999, March 2000

ISBN: 0-926902-54-7

INCENTIVE COMPENSATION

and Employee Ownership

THIRD EDITION

Edited by Scott S. Rodrick

The National Center for Employee Ownership
Oakland, California

Incentive Compensation and Employee Ownership
Editing and design by Scott S. Rodrick

The National Center for Employee Ownership
1736 Franklin Street, 8th Floor, Oakland, CA 94612
(510) 208-1300
(510) 272-9510 (fax)
E-mail: *nceo@nceo.org*
Web site: *http://www.nceo.org/*

First edition (under the title *Incentive Compensation for Employee Ownership Companies*) published February 1998

Second edition November 1998

Third edition May 1999; reprinted October 1999, March 2000

ISBN: 0-926902-54-7

Contents

Preface

This book discusses incentive compensation—i.e., compensation in the form of a reward for improved individual, group, or company performance. Such plans, which may range from cash bonuses to stock options, form a vital part of the business practices of many companies. In today's competitive business environment, more and more companies are finding that more and more employees are crucial to overall corporate performance; consequently, many of these companies are using incentive compensation to retain employees and encourage them to increase productivity.

Incentive plans relate to employee ownership (i.e., ownership of company stock by employees) in two ways. First, the incentive plan itself may be in the form of stock, in which case it frequently takes the form of a stock option plan (see, e.g., chapter 5, "Performance-Based Stock Options"). Second, the short-term rewards of incentive compensation can fill a gap left by a longer-term benefit such as an employee stock ownership plan (ESOP) (see, e.g., the discussion in chapter 2 under the heading "Do Short-Term Incentives Make Ownership Real?").

Although this book covers stock options at various points (e.g., in chapters 4, 5, and 9), it is not a book about stock options or any other plan per se. Rather, the focus is on the incentive concept and what you can do with it. Other books, such as our publication *The Stock Options Book*, describe all the technicalities of particular types of plans. The diversity of plans described in these pages matches the diversity of plans you will find in various companies. It is common to find more than one type of stock or cash incentive plan; see, for example, chapter 9, "Incentive Compensation and Employee Ownership at SAIC."

Readers should recognize that what works for one situation may not work for another, but that at the same time meaningless, feel-good slogans about empowering employees will not fill the bill. An effective incentive plan needs to be specific and customized for each particular situation. You probably will not find an exact blueprint for your company's plan in the following pages; you will, however, find a wealth of information, ideas, and inspiration on how to proceed. We hope that some of these ideas will fit your situation or, more likely, will stimulate you to think of some new combinations of ideas that will work.

The chapters in this book fall into two basic categories. First, the chapters in Part One, "Essays," introduce readers to the field of incentive compensation and describe how various plans, both stock- and cash-based, work for various companies. Second, the chapters in Part Two, "Case Studies," illustrate how specific companies have implemented specific plans. There is necessarily some overlap between the two categories, as when Jack Stack illustrates the concepts in Chapter 3 with examples from his company, or when William Scott describes what his company does in Chapter 9 and then recommends what other companies should do.

Much of the material here originally appeared in the winter 1997 issue of the *Journal of Employee Ownership Law and Finance*, the only serious journal devoted to employee ownership. The second edition of this book added chapters 5 and 7, and this third edition adds chapter 6.

For more information about equity incentives and what we at the National Center for Employee Ownership (NCEO) offer, see our Web site at *www.nceo.org* or call us at (510) 272-9461.

Part One

Essays

Measuring, Improving, and Rewarding Performance

Jerry McAdams

It has taken us 80 years since the Industrial Revolution to discover the customer and about 90 to discover employees. And discover them we have. We have figured out how to calculate the lifetime value of a customer and are trying to figure out the value of employee contributions to the success of our organizations. Just how important employees are to the company is being brought home to us through this book. It provides us with practices that have been developed and tested, practices that are making a difference.

Use Every Asset You Have

Competitiveness demands getting the best possible return on an organization's assets. If you believe people are assets and not solely a cost of doing business, this book shows you ways of getting a better return on these employed assets. In addition to base pay, many organizations are spending a good deal of money, time, and energy on all kinds of compensation, reward, and recognition plans

---

Mr. McAdams adapted portions of this chapter from his book *The Reward Plan Advantage: A Manager's Guide to Improving Business Performance Through People* (San Francisco, CA: Jossey-Bass, 1996).

with little understanding of what they are getting back. If they try to understand what they get back, sometimes they can put a dollar value on their return. Sometimes they can't. (It may make good business sense even without a dollar return.) In either case, when organizations want employees to make a difference, they must be clear on their objectives and make the plans *positively reinforcing* to employees. In addition, if we want to maximize that return, organizations must have the courage to unleash the creative energy of employees, enabling them to become contributing stakeholders. This process of involving employees as contributing stakeholders is being successfully applied in every type of organization—service, manufacturing, union, non-union, private and public. For many, it is the *way they operate the organization*.

The Reinforcement Model

Most of us have a basic understanding of how pay systems work. We are probably not going to change the fundamental way we pay people. Therefore, the focus is on a better understanding of what we get from these systems now and how we can use additional (or redirected) funds to launch plans more directly aligned with your organization's objectives.

It is helpful to put these plans in context through a reinforcement model (figure 1-1). *Business Objectives and Desired Culture* drive the design of reinforcement systems, characterized as *compensation, capability, recognition, group incentive,* and *project team incentive* plans. These characterizations are ordered from left to right in figure 1-1 according to their contribution to results—the degree to which one can attribute performance improvement to the plan. The two ends of the continuum are labeled "cost of doing business"—*compensation* (base pay, benefits, and most adjustments to base pay)—and "business results"—*project team incentive* plans that reward only when the result of the contribution is measurable and valuable. The more one moves from left to right, the more directly one can attribute the business result to the reward plan.

Moving from left to right also moves from an administrative mindset to a creative one. Beginning at *capability* plans, the creative

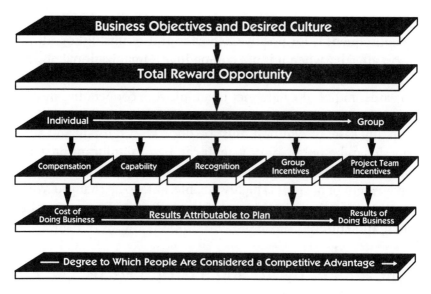

Figure 1-1. The reinforcement model

demand from an organization focuses on imaginative approaches in a constantly changing environment. It describes an increasing opportunity for alignment between all employees and those objectives that determine organizational success. It deals with the ability of an organization to meet those objectives in a cost-effective manner. It can open up the systems to allow employees to move from job-bound, narrowly focused, micro-managed cost centers to enabled corporate contributors with both accountability and reward. Issues of goal setting; coaching and feedback; performance appraisal; and pay for knowledge, skill, and competencies are those of *capability*.

Recognition as the Organizationally Approved "Thank You"

Recognition plans are after the fact, by definition. They are not "do this and you will get that," but "we saw you do this and thanks for doing it." Whenever possible, think as recognition as the WD-40 oil of all interventions. It smoothes the way for all performance improvement by creating and reinforcing an environment of positive consequences for positive behavior and results. Recognition is most effective when it is not competitive. Organizational objectives are rarely met by employees competing for a limited number of awards; rather, they are met by employees cooperating in the best interests of all.

In any case, recognition must be done with honesty and sincerity. It can be public or private. It can be of significant or symbolic value. It can recognize individuals or groups. It can come from management or peers. It is highly flexible, able to be changed from month to month, objective to objective. But it always must be honest and sincere.

Improvement by Adding a Group Focus

Most managers have been taught to believe that proper administration of compensation plans is their only weapon and that it can (or should) do it all. I disagree.

We already know a good deal about improving performance by focusing on the individual employee. This practice assumes that improvement of every person's performance (assuming one could measure it) will roll up to organizational improvement. While that may be the case, we will never know for sure if it works. With the possible exception of sales, we cannot prove that a 10% improvement in individual productivity, as an example, will result in a cumulative 10% productivity gain for the entire organization—or any gain at all, for that matter. Accounting, measurement, job, and operational systems are too complex for such a simplistic approach.

Competitiveness demands engaging all employees in making a business successful. That demands that everyone know, understand, focus, and act on those objectives that determine organizational success. Group incentive and project team incentive plans, in the broadest terms, are designed expressly to improve organizational success.

At a conference in San Francisco, one of my audience members argued against rewarding everyone in a group for improving performance. He didn't believe a file clerk could influence the measures. I pointed out he was right—if you just see the person as a file clerk, confined to filing. But if you view the clerk as an intelligent human being and allow him or her to contribute, he could make a difference. Our challenge is to enable that file clerk to collaborate with others to make a contribution and be rewarded for the result or recognized for the effort.

Group incentives are distinguished from project team incentives by the definition of "group." In this case, it means an organizational unit—a workgroup, department, division, business unit, or entire company. A project team does not appear on the organizational chart. It can be two people in the same workgroup or a cross-functional team assembled for a specific purpose. In either the group or project team incentive plans, the focus is on results of the group or team and not on individual contributions. Mixing the focus reduces the effectiveness of the plans. You can have plans designed specifically for individuals that work nicely along the side of group or team-based plans.

An additional goal of these plans is to create an environment that unleashes the creativity of employees. That creativity, when channeled through clear direction and enabling processes, is one of our most effective competitive elements.

It's Not All About Reinforcement

I do not believe that individual compensation, recognition, and reward plans are the *only* way to improve an organization's performance. Far from it. Financial literacy, organizational redesign, re-engineering, systems and process development, new products and services, quality, becoming "customer-driven," along with hiring, orientation, and career development practices and all kinds of other interventions are destined to affect performance.

Reinforcement systems can lead the improvement process or lag it, but they absolutely must reinforce it. The problem is that most experts in these other disciplines mentioned in the paragraph above only pay lip service to reinforcement, and that is a lost opportunity. Those of us who have participated in our umpteenth management by objective (MBO) process, without reinforcement, know what I mean. I believe what gets measured gets managed, and what gets rewarded gets done.

Another caveat: I believe in intrinsic rewards as well as extrinsic. We need both. No reward plan will offset a lousy supervisor who makes your job painful. Nor will it offset a job you hate. By the same token, to rely solely on intrinsic rewards is a mistake. It doesn't take long for employees to say, "I really like working on this special team to improve the process, but what else is in it for me?" As with all things, we must strike a balance.

As my father, a tough Depression-age realist, used to say, "If you want to get people really involved, get them to put some skin in the game." In this context, "skin" is employees sharing risk *and* reward with the organization in the game of business.

I suggest that you review the case studies included here as thought-starters and "tales from the trenches." They are not to be replicated but instead adapted to your organizational needs. With the proper use of this information, you can be better prepared to meet the challenges of an increasingly competitive marketplace.

Beyond Bribery: Communicating Short-Term Group Incentives

Cathy Ivancic

"Eat your vegetables and you can have dessert," the old saying goes. Does this extrinsic reward—dessert—really motivate anyone to eat vegetables? I know that my child complies with this "incentive" by jamming the remaining zucchini into his mouth and swallowing hard. I did the same to my parents when they offered me this incentive. (Perhaps you did too.) Obviously, the reward did not create a full understanding of the need for the behavior, nor did it develop a desire to repeat it in the future. No, the "dessert" incentive engendered only temporary compliance, not a real "ownership" of the process.

Creating incentives that encourage an ownership mentality can be a challenge. Employee-owned companies often turn to short-term group incentives to provide current benefits for owners, stimulate a deeper sense of ownership, and build knowledge about the business. But what makes short-term group incentives in employee-owned companies any different from the classic vegetable bribe?

Even incentives implemented for the right reasons can be perceived by employees as meaningless or manipulative. The challenge, of course, is getting beyond bribery. Proper incentive design is a starting point, but the ultimate success of an incentive is rooted in how it is communicated and implemented. This chapter, by describing the experiences of three companies with success in this area and providing specific ideas for improving communication approaches, illustrates how the communication of short-term incentives can enhance their effectiveness.

Do Short-Term Incentives Make Ownership Real?

Employee ownership's greatest strength—a shared interest in long-term performance—is also its greatest weakness. For younger employees and people who are not familiar with the benefits of equity ownership, the rewards can seem nonexistent. Equity ownership has drawbacks as an incentive. First, the rewards are not timely, and second, the connection to daily work is difficult to see. This is particularly true where the value of the equity is realized at retirement, such as in an employee stock ownership plan (ESOP). In ESOP companies, incentives are frequently implemented to make ownership more "real." If you reward people for current performance results, so the thinking goes, they will be more aware of how the business is doing and pay attention to performance.

Among the strongest advocates of short-term incentives are companies that describe themselves as "open-book" firms. These companies point to their bonus programs as linchpins of their successful approach.[1] Open-book advocate Jack Stack, president of Springfield ReManufacturing Corporation, summed it up this way: "What a bonus program does is communicate goals in the most effective way possible—by putting a bounty on them."[2]

But this positive experience with incentives is not universal. In fact, many employee-owned companies are disappointed with the results of their incentive programs. The story often goes something like this: XYZ company has an annual bonus tied to performance such as a percentage of annual net income. In addition, employees also have the long-term benefit of employee ownership. Despite these clear incentives, people do not act in ways that earn the bonus or grow stock value. Leaders at XYZ company have posted reports and provided information on the incentive with little results from the apathetic work force. Like children who resist eating vegetables, the employee owners do not know what is good for them.

Research on rewards supports this notion that rewards can backfire and fail to cultivate an understanding of group purpose. The critics of incentives—including leading organizational thinkers such as W. Edwards Deming—say that rewards can encourage short-term thinking, nourish rivalries, and even damage teamwork.[3] These negative analyses are most strongly targeted at individual merit pay-for-performance plans, but critiques are also leveled against group incentives such as profit sharing plans and group bonus systems. Rosabeth Moss Kanter notes that variable incentives are often unconnected to what employees contribute and may put a large part of compensation at risk—a problem for lower-paid employees who cannot afford to take that chance.[4] In *Punished by Rewards*, Alfie Kohn characterizes incentives as manipulations that cultivate shortsighted behavior, encourage orchestration of appearances, and distract from the intrinsic value of doing good work. Kohn argues that even group rewards can muster only "temporary compliance" and will eventually be seen as manipulation.[5] Peter Block contends—in his 1993 critique of traditional corporate governance—that despite the popular belief to the contrary, the research on rewards indicates that "productivity is not for sale."[6]

Designing Group Incentives

Many problems with group incentives result from one or more of the following design flaws, which inhibit the plan's effectiveness:

- Incentives create too much focus on one goal (e.g., production) at the expense of another (e.g., quality).
- Incentives reward the wrong behavior for the objectives of the plan.
- They are discretionary (at a supervisor or board's discretion).
- The plan is too complex for the group's level of knowledge.
- The incentive is not calculated frequently enough (monthly is better than annually).

- The payment does not vary.
- The plan rewards individual performance, thereby creating competition where teamwork is needed.
- The incentive is not tied to company-wide performance.
- Employee efforts are not connected to the reward.
- The incentive is not self-funding.

A challenge of incentive design is the fact that there are necessary tradeoffs. When a plan is simple and tied to company-wide goals, it is often not clearly related to things employees control. On the other hand, an incentive linked to department or team performance, which is easy to understand, may miss the mark regarding the company's general performance. When incentives are tied to a purely objective calculation, they may not take into account subjective measures that are important for the future success of the company. Because of these tradeoffs, the search for the perfect incentive formula can be a futile one. In fact, many of the companies that describe their incentives as outstanding successes technically suffer from one or more of the above design flaws.

Attention to design can avoid creating insurmountable obstacles, but the success of group incentives ultimately rests on the effectiveness of the processes used to implement and communicate them. Good design cannot overcome poor communication, but good communication can overcome flaws caused by tradeoffs in the design process.

Communicating Short-Term Incentives

The three employee-owned companies highlighted in this chapter describe their incentive programs as a 6 or higher on a scale of 1 to 10 in terms of reaching their intended objectives.[7] The design elements of these successful short-term incentives vary tremendously, but the communication of the plans have the following common characteristics. Each of the three companies found a way for the incentive to be "owned" by employees, linked it to growing knowledge of business objectives, and created ways for people to make improvements in the business.

Bimba Manufacturing: Keeping Track and Growing Knowledge of "Our" Business

"I don't do my job to get the bonus. I'm from the old school where you are expected to do a good job. The bonus just helps me know how well we are doing," says Brian Cash, a maintenance leader at Bimba Manufacturing in Monee, Illinois. Similarly, his coworker Joyce Greep explains that she will gladly accept higher performance goals "because I'm proud of my company and want to serve customers." For Greep and Cash, the incentive is an indicator of how *their company* is doing rather than an exercise in satisfying company leaders. This buy-in by employees—achieved more by implementation than by design—is an essential ingredient in the success of a group incentive.

The objectives of the Bimba incentive plan are to broaden the understanding of customer requirements, share rewards, and build a sense of purpose. "We have a written vision statement, but the incentives reinforce our purpose and keep the focus," notes Dennis Damrow, vice president of operations at the employee-owned manufacturer of pneumatic actuators.

Group incentives for the 450 employee owners at Bimba Manufacturing come in several forms. The company calculates a quarterly bonus based on exceeding performance targets. When targets are exceeded, everyone in the company can earn up to 10% of compensation in a bonus. Sixty percent of that amount is contingent on company-wide profitability targets. The other 40% is contingent on reaching specific workgroup targets. The workgroup targets focus on the specific function of a department. For example, a department may have local targets related to customer service, work order completion, and safety. In order for someone in that department to get their full bonus, the company-wide target and the local targets must be met.

Bonus payments have been generated often, but they are not

guaranteed. For example, two years ago the program paid in only two of the four quarters. Last year there were payments every quarter.

In addition to the bonus described above, Bimba has a separate customer service bonus that can be paid quarterly. This bonus—a flat $250 per person—is contingent on meeting targets on product request dates and promise dates. The company recently initiated a new way of tracking this bonus. Rather than paying $250 when the summarized quarterly targets are met, the targets are tracked weekly. When each weekly target is met, $20 is added to that quarter's customer service bonus.

Company leaders and employees agree that the incentives have contributed to improved performance. Bimba has significantly outpaced the industry in volume growth. In addition, the company received Class A MRP-II (customer service) certification in January 1996. The bonus program's most significant effect has been to focus a greater number of people on customer requirements. Customer service targets have been increased in each of the past four years, with current targets at 97% of promise dates and 90% of request dates.

Incentives are communicated in a variety of ways at Bimba. The company makes use of conventional communication methods, including annual meetings, newsletters, and posting of results. Departments select their own methods to share results, including postings, meetings, and one-on-one conversations.

Bimba also makes use of some uncommon approaches. The incentives are included in the company's week-long orientation for new employees. It is one of the 16 different sessions provided. New employees also learn about benefits, the company's markets, diversity, problem-solving, and the company's ESOP. The message for new employees is clear: these incentives are part of this company's overall business strategy, and it is very important that everyone in the company understand that strategy.

The ongoing tracking and communication of the customer service measure takes place weekly. Each Monday a cross-functional group of managers and schedulers meets to review the week's performance. The meeting, run by the sales and marketing department, provides current information to the rest of the company about performance on customer service targets. The information in the Monday meeting is brought back to each workgroup. Weekly tracking reveals the effect that events and different departments have on the numbers. The way local targets are set is also part of the communication process.

Setting local targets is an exercise in helping people connect their department to the company's objectives. Leaders in each department are asked to identify the things they do in their area that help reach the company-wide goals. They make a proposal, and the departmental activities are turned into targets that quantify their connection, with guidance from top-level leaders. The process of talking about and setting targets is an education for everyone involved on how all the pieces fit together to meet company goals. "That (the communication about goals) is the real benefit," according to Damrow.

On the surface, the Bimba Manufacturing incentives seem complex and difficult to understand. However, in the context of how the incentive evolved, it becomes clear that current incentives are the result of a multi-year educational process. Today's bonuses came about as company leaders changed the incentive each year to fit with current objectives and the growing sophistication of employee owners.

Each modification helped people to learn about new elements of their business. When the company first established the ESOP, discretionary bonuses were paid. Looking for a better link to performance, the quarterly incentive was established in 1989. The first incentive bonus was simple; it was paid if the company as a whole exceeded profitability targets. A few years later, the customer service measures were included as part of the company-wide goals. In the following year, the customer service incentive was broken out as a separate bonus paid equally to each person, and the other bonus remained a percentage of pay. In recent years, the local incentives were added as part of the criteria for the bonus based on compensation.

In this evolutionary context, Bimba's local incentives are reflections of the overall company goals rather than distinct departmental rewards. The two-way conversation about how each work area contributes to the company's goals connects local incentives to the common goals. "It works like a relay team," says Greep, "If we find that they [workers in another department] aren't making their bonus, we'll figure out how we can pass the baton better to help them get it."

The range of incentives and the changing targets at Bimba Manufacturing help people learn more about their company and what helps improve its performance. The two-way communication about targets and the frequency of that communication have created incentives that are tools for continuous improvement rather than carrots for behavior.

Zandex: Employee Owners Create Their Own Incentive

"I like to describe it as the 'birthing process,'" says Kurt Southam, president of Zandex Health Care Corporation, when talking about employee participation in developing incentives. At this Ohio chain of nursing and retirement homes, nearly 1000 employees had opportunities to comment, critique, and modify a proposed incentive plan. This "gestation period," according to Southam, helped people to support the end result. In a sense, the long process of feedback and redraft helped make the incentives their "baby."

One of the Zandex incentives—the Committed Owners of Zandex program (COZ)—creates a special set of rewards for employees who are committed to the company mission. The company's mission, which was developed several years before the incentive plan, is "to provide compassionate, responsible care for residents which will provide security for the employees and profitability for the shareholders." At Zandex, employees are shareholders, with 25% of the shares in an ESOP.

The COZ program came about as a result of discussions initiated by company leaders about the obstacles to accomplishing the company's mission. One of the obstacles employee owners identified was the lack of a way to reward people who consistently supported the company's mission.

All employees were asked to comment in writing and in small groups on the best way to reward these "exceptional people" and also to help develop criteria for selecting who these people are. The rewards selected were extra personal days, vacation days, an automatic attendance bonus, and an extra grade at the top of the pay scale. There were five rounds of comments and ideas collected from employees on various drafts of the proposed program. A high percentage of employees shared ideas on the plan.

Through this process, employees selected the criteria for who was a "committed owner." A COZ employee is judged on the following criteria: attendance, flexibility, initiative, professionalism, teamwork, company commitment, and grooming. To become eligible for the program, an employee is recommended by his or her supervisor and required to pass a short test about company policies and employee ownership. The test is changed each year. If an employee's performance has remained good, he or she is invited to take another version of the test on company philosophy and policies to enter the program again.

The COZ program was put to a vote by each of the company's eight locations. Employee owners voted in proportion to the shares in their ESOP accounts (participants with no shares were given five votes). All but one location passed the final proposal by an 80% positive vote. The program was implemented in all facilities except for that one location. Employee owners at this facility sent a clear message that—at the time of the vote—this incentive was not "their baby." Later that year, employees of that facility voted to have the COZ program (90% wanted it).

After one year of the program, approximately 40% of employees are COZ employees. This program, along with the other incentives at Zandex, has contributed to cutting absenteeism in half and significantly reducing turnover.

Zandex has used this process of employee commentary to arrive at policies on company issues and incentives. Voting on nearly all policy changes, employee owners at Zandex have a direct say in changes that directly affect their work life.

The company has a bonus based on company profitability that is paid every six months. Three years ago, the company proposed to reduce the bonus checks of people with excessive "call-offs" (absenteeism resulting from the employee calling in sick or with an excuse); attendance is a recurring problem in this industry, where the jobs are emotionally challenging and turnover is high. Employees voted on both the number of acceptable "call offs" and later on whether it would result in a reduction or a complete forfeiture of the bonus. The group voted to have employees who have excessive "call offs" forfeit their bonus completely and reallocate that money to other employees.

Without the "birthing process," these incentive programs can resemble the kind of reward critics say will create divisions and erode teamwork. The programs make distinctions between individuals based on merit, and COZ has subjective judgment by supervisors. But the employees themselves said that such distinctions were necessary to support Zandex's mission. Through the process, employees tinkered with the program to help minimize its design tradeoffs and still accomplish its objectives. Employee owners came to "own" the incentive by having a chance to shape it.

Floturn: Awareness Through Formal and Informal Communication

When you come to work at Floturn, an employee-owned manufacturer in Cincinnati, Ohio, you need to understand the bonus system to take the job. Without understanding it, you will not know whether you are being compensated adequately. Base pay is typically just below market rates at this manufacturer of laser printer and photocopier substrates. It is the bonus program that makes it a good-paying job. The bonus, which has been in existence since 1971, typically pays anywhere from 75% to 125% of annual compensation each year.

The bonus pool is one-third of company profits. "One-third goes to the bonus pool, one-third goes back into the company, and one-third goes to taxes," explains Art Scharinger, company treasurer. The annualized bonus is paid on a quarterly basis. The pool is paid to employee owners as a percentage of compensation. In early quarters, a percentage of the quarterly calculation is reserved to offset the possibility of poor performance in future quarters. By the end of the year, the full one-third of profits is paid out.

Floturn consistently pays bonuses. "There was only one year, 1986, when we didn't pay any bonus," says Scharinger. The amounts of the bonuses, however, vary with company performance, from as low as 6.5% of pay in the early years to well over 100% in recent years.

Company officials feel that the company's ESOP, which owns more than 80% of the company's stock, provides a hedge against shortsighted thinking that might be created by this kind of incentive. The bonus is designed to work with the ESOP, providing short-term gains for employee owners who will not realize equity (i.e., ESOP) benefits until retirement.

The bonus has helped to build awareness about company performance and help people understand how everyday work affects it. For example, a machine operator pointed out that moving another machine closer to his workstation would enable him to run two machines simultaneously. "Without the bonus, we would not have seen that kind of awareness, " noted Scharinger. This awareness is combined with a management style that assumes that people can make improvements in the business and encourages them to do so.

As a result of the business awareness, people have made corrections that have reduced costs, such as reducing scrap and cutting back the hours they work. These efforts—combined with a fast-growing market—have led to outstanding corporate performance. Floturn's stock value has increased more than 1,080% in less than an eight-year period. The company has outperformed the industry in growth. When the industry grew 16%, Floturn grew 30%.

Communication about the bonus program starts before you even work at Floturn. It begins with your first introduction to the company, which is likely to be from a family member who works there. Exposure to information about the bonus continues through employee orientation and quarterly meetings about the bonus. Each quarter the company has a meeting where the financial results are shared and the bonus is announced. The meeting is on paid time. Each month of the quarter there is some communication about the bonus; in the first month there is the quarterly meeting, a month later people get the check, and the following month the next quarter closes.

On top of the formal communication, there are many informal ways people learn about how they affect business performance. When the company first became employee-owned, only a small group of 33 people worked at the facility. With the small size and a relatively flat organization, the company established a tradition of leaders responding to questions about performance and helping people see the connection to their jobs.

As the company grows (it now employs nearly 140 people), informal communication continues to be an important part of how people learn about the business. "Most people are related to someone here," says Scharinger. "Old-timers tell the newcomers how our work affects the bonus." In addition, because such a large part of compensation is tied to performance, employees may have to explain the bonus to people outside the company. For example, the company helps employees explain the compensation system to lenders when employee owners want to buy a house.

While some companies achieve their educational objectives by changing the bonus, Floturn has instead achieved an educational impact by keeping it the same. The longevity of the bonus, the regularized communication, and the size of the payouts has created an incentive system that is well known and valued by employee owners.

An Incentive People Can Call Their Own

Employee ownership companies may have an advantage over conventionally owned companies because the long-term benefit of equity ownership balances short-term thinking created by an incentive plan. Ownership may create a foundation for seeing the incentive as a step toward a shared goal rather than a manipulative practice. As Frank Hudetz, the CEO of Solar Press, an employee-owned company in Naperville, Illinois, writes, "long-term incentives tied to company philosophy can prove worthy of the highest employee performance and build intrinsic motivation—the highest order of incentive."[8]

Most of the research suggests that employee ownership alone, without employee participation, does not create this "highest order of incentive."[9] In companies like those described above, the implementation and communication of the short-term incentives are key elements in effective participation. Properly communicated and implemented incentives provide a focus for working toward common goals.

The companies in this chapter have not discovered the perfect group incentive formula. Each incentive has its design tradeoffs. Bimba Manufacturing is an elaborate plan that can be complex to understand. Zandex's COZ program relies on subjective measures that could be seen as favoritism. Floturn's bonus based on profitability is not tied directly to job-level improvements. If you took any one of these incentive designs and transplanted them into another company, the incentive would have a high likelihood of failure. Design is not the common denominator in their success. It is the way they have implemented the design that makes them work.

Each of the companies uses a communication process in which the methods and the tone send a strong message about who is in charge of the incentive. The incentive is not perceived by employees as management's effort to change their behavior; instead, it is a scorecard to show people how they are doing. In addition, these companies are clear about how the incentive fits with the group's shared objectives. The specific communication processes chosen are different, but they have following common characteristics:

Employees, not company leaders, "own" the process. When people talk about group incentives in these companies, they describe it as something the group can influence. The incentive is not a reward bestowed on employees by leaders or a carrot to motivate employees. Leaders do not dish out the rewards. Instead, it is a way of keeping track of shared performance.

Incentives are part of building knowledge about business objectives. Successful group incentives are not stand-alone programs, they are expressions of business objectives. These incentives find their way into regularized communications, formal education sessions, and informal dialogue about work. These incentives are part of reaching common objectives and learning how to do that better. One of their key functions is to teach people about how the company makes money.

People get more than material rewards. Social and emotional rewards come from the fact that people are empowered to affect results. Working together to achieve the reward, using one's creativity to solve problems, and being a part of reaching objectives are personally rewarding. The way an incentive is implemented can help or hinder its ability to generate these nonmaterial rewards for people.

Methods to Help Improve Communication About Group Incentives

Identifying these common characteristics of success is not a useful exercise without practical ideas about the actions that help create these results. What can companies do to improve their communication about incentives? The ideas below, based on the experiences of more than 50 employee-owned companies throughout the United States that use incentives, can provide a starting point for companies working to improve their communication about incentives.[10]

Include both numbers and the stories behind the numbers. Develop the skills of leaders throughout your company to communicate about performance in both numbers and stories. Group incentives tied to measurable results are not useful if people do not understand how the measure fits with daily work. Stories paint the picture of how work and the performance numbers fit together. The art of telling the business story must be cultivated throughout the company.

Provide an opportunity for people at all levels to tell their own stories. Top-level leaders need to work to relinquish the job of explaining why the incentive went up or down. Employees must to develop the knowledge and information needed to be able to tell their own stories. Leaders should challenge them to do this by turning the communication about performance into a two-way conversation and creating regular opportunities for the conversation to take place. If your company chooses to do formal training on business concepts, make sure the educational approach goes beyond a standard lecture-style format and challenges people to practice talking about their contribution to performance.

Run communication on a frequent and regular schedule. If an employee only hears about the bonus at the annual meeting, it is difficult to see the connection to daily work. Regularized communications (quarterly, monthly, or even weekly) help make the incentive a point of focus for daily activities. Moreover, they provide the repetition needed for learning to take place.

Educate people on how their work affects the numbers. Teach people about how they affect performance. Teaching about company financial statements is not enough. Focus educational efforts—both those that happen in a classroom and regularized company communications—on creating a "line of sight" (i.e., a clearly perceptible connection) between daily work and company performance. Developing a common language for talking about these connections is much more important than knowledge of financial statements.

Set objectives for your incentive and invite employees to participate in the process. If there are not clear goals for the incentive plan, it is time to think again about whether one is needed. Asking employees to help define the goals of the incentive, set the criteria, or establish local objectives helps people "own" the results.

Create opportunities for employees to make improvements that affect performance. Without avenues for employee participation, an incentive cannot be a way to focus actions. Consider the following approaches to excessive overtime. One approach is to set a company limit on available overtime and explain that it is in everyone's interest because it is eating into the bonus. A second approach would be to explain how overtime is connected to the bonus and challenge employees to make suggestions and implement changes in the things that contribute to excessive overtime. In the first example, the incentive is a justification for a company policy. In the second example, the incentive is evidence that employees can affect performance. A group incentive is empty without genuine empowerment to make improvements.

Make it fun and engaging. Who made the rule that communication about company performance must be boring and dull? Most of the traditional means for communicating about performance— annual reports, shareholder meetings, or reviews of the financial statements—were originally designed for outsiders. Meeting targets is fun; overcoming business challenges is exciting; working together toward common goals is rewarding. Unfortunately, most companies do not make their communication about these things reflect that excitement. When communicating with insiders, it is fine to break the "rules" by making it into a game, using visual aids and props, making noise, singing, or even jumping up on your chair. Consider that communicating about performance is not much different from other ways of keeping score for a group. An announcer at a football game would never say, "on page six of the handout you'll see the detailed graph that shows Central High has improved yards gained in the second quarter." Keep score on a big board where everyone can see and get employee owners involved in providing the high-energy commentary.

Beyond Bribery: Who Owns the Results in Your Company?

Short-term group incentives do not always develop a sense of purpose or an "ownership" of the work process. The implementation and communication of group incentives can make a tremendous difference in whether employee owners see the incentive as manipulation—like the "vegetable bribe"—or as a tool for self-improvement. When employee owners believe that leaders are in control of the game (as in a parent-child relationship), incentives will create temporary compliance at best. When employee owners do not understand their business and its objectives, incentives cannot help achieve the business objectives. Finally, unless extrinsic incentives help people to track and control their own activities, the reward will not help people to take "ownership" of the results of their work.

Notes

1. See John Case, *Open-Book Management: The Coming Business Revolution,* (New York: HarperCollins, 1995), and John P. Schuster, Jill Carpenter, and M. Patricia Kane, *The Power of Open-Book Management* (New York: John Wiley & Sons, Inc., 1996) for detailed examples of companies that describe the incentive component of their company culture as an important element of their success.

2. Jack Stack and Bo Burlingham, *The Great Game of Business* (New York: Currency Doubleday, 1992), 122. [Editor's note: The relevant chapter in Stack's book is excerpted in chapter 3 of this book.]

3. W. Edwards Deming, *Out of the Crisis* (Cambridge: MIT Center for Advanced Engineering Study, 1986), 102. See also Fredrick Herzberg, "One More Time: How Do You Motivate Employees?" *Harvard Business Review,* January/February 1968, 53–62. Herzberg maintains the answer to this question is that "you don't."

4. See Rosabeth Moss Kanter, *When Giants Learn to Dance* (New York: Simon and Schuster, 1989), 234–237.

5. Alfie Kohn, *Punished by Rewards: The Trouble with Gold Stars, Incentive Plans, A's, Praise, and Other Bribes* (New York: Houghton Mifflin Company, 1993).

6. See Peter S. Block, *Stewardship: Choosing Service over Self-Interest* (San Francisco: Berrett Koehler Publishers, 1993), 167.

7. Descriptions are based on conversations with company leaders and formal interviews completed in fall 1996.

8. See Frank C. Hudetz," Self-Actualization and Self-Esteem Are the Highest Order of Incentives," at the Foundation for Enterprise Development's World Wide Web site at *http://www.fed.org/.*

9. Employee ownership alone is not correlated with improved corporate performance. See General Accounting Office, *Employee Ownership Plans:*

Little Evidence of Effects on Corporate Performance (Washington, D.C.: GAO/PEMD-88-1, 1987).

10. See Cathy Ivancic and Jim Bado, *Open-Book Management: Getting Started* (Menlo Park, CA: Crisp Publications, 1997).

Incentive Compensation and the Great Game of Business

Jack Stack

There is no more powerful tool a manager can have than a good bonus program—which is why some companies will pay a consultant tens of thousands of dollars to design one. That's not necessarily a stupid investment. If a bonus program works, it can be an incredible motivator. It can get people producing at levels that make the cost of the program seem like peanuts, no matter how much you may have spent to set it up.

What a bonus program does is communicate goals in the most effective way possible—by putting a bounty on them. It says to people, "These targets are so important, we'll give you a reward if you hit them." When you do that, you get people's attention very fast. You send them a strong message. You provide them with a focus. You give them a challenge and a very good reason for working as hard and as smart as they can to meet it: they're going to get paid. In "the Great Game of Business" (the "Game"), we get all that and much, much more from our bonus program, and we didn't pay anyone a dime to come up with it. We call it "Skip the

---

Mr. Stack adapted this chapter from his and Bo Burlingham's book *The Great Game of Business* (New York: Currency Books, 1992), chapter 7, "Skip The Praise—Give Us the Raise."

Praise—Give Us the Raise," or STP-GUTR—pronounced Stop-Gooter. Following are some of the things we like about it.

Stop-Gooter is our most effective educational program. We use it to teach people about business. If the goal is to improve the debt-equity ratio, people learn about debt and equity and how they affect both. The same holds for pretax profits, or inventory accuracy, or the overhead charge-out rate. Whatever the goal, it gives people a big incentive to find out about some aspect of the accounting system, the company, and the competitive environment. Otherwise they won't have much fun, they won't earn the bonus, and they'll take a lot of flak from their peers.

The bonus program serves as a kind of insurance policy on the company and our jobs. That's because we use it to target our vulnerabilities. Every year, we figure out what the greatest threat the company faces is, and we get the entire work force to go after it in the bonus program. In effect, we put an annual bounty on fixing our weaknesses. That gives everyone an additional reason to achieve the goals. These are musts, not wants, and so they are worth the extra effort. Interestingly enough, once a weakness is fixed, it tends to say fixed.

The program brings us together as a team. It ensures that everyone has the same priorities and that we all stay focused on the same goals. It eliminates mixed messages. When one department is having trouble, another department will send in reinforcements, and everybody understands why. Often, people don't even have to be asked. They will help each other out spontaneously, sometimes at great inconvenience. That's because the program makes everyone aware of how much we depend on one another to hit our targets. We win together or we don't win at all.

The program helps us identify problems fast. If we don't achieve a goal, we find out very quickly why we missed it. Everybody is looking through the numbers to see what the problem is. Maybe it's receivables: customers are slowing down their payments and conserving cash. Maybe it's productivity: people are new in their jobs and can't absorb overhead fast enough. The bonus program forces the problem out into the open. Once it's there, you can go to work on it. You can solve it.

Stop-Gooter is the best tool we have for increasing the value of our stock. We always set it up to guarantee the stock value will rise substantially if we hit our targets—and will be protected even if we don't. That's one of the most important messages we send through the program: "This Game is all about equity and job security." Short-term incentives like bonuses are fine, but we want to make sure people never lose sight of the long-term payoff.

Most importantly, the bonus program provides the structure of the Game. It puts the ball in play. It sets the tempo. It keeps the action going week in, week out, all year long. It gives us a language, a way of communicating. It creates excitement, anticipation. It gets the adrenaline flowing. It makes sure that people stay involved, engaged, on their toes. It is, in short, our most important motivator, which is its primary function. If it weren't raising the energy level, we'd stop using it, although I find it hard to imagine how it could fail to motivate. That's a question we constantly pose: "Is the bonus program motivating people?" But I have to admit that if anybody ever told me it wasn't, I'd think that he was a dirty liar— or that our education program was in deep trouble.

Bootstrapping: The Best Reason for Paying People with Bonuses

I am a strong believer in operating a company, any company, as if its future were always on the line, as if something could happen at any moment to threaten its survival. Most companies do, in fact, follow that principle when they are starting up. They don't take the future for granted because they can't. They know that they could run out of cash next week and the game would be over. So they become extremely resourceful. They constantly look for an edge, for ways to cut costs and save money, for things they can do to get more bang for their buck. It's known as bootstrapping, and it's how every business should be run, not just startups. Bootstrapping is a mentality, a set of habits, and a way of operating based on self-reliance, ingenuity, intelligence, and hard work. When you don't bootstrap, you grow fat and sloppy. You get into the habit of buying solutions to your problems. You take the future for granted. You assume you'll be in business forever. You let your costs rise, and you take your eye off the ball. You get caught up in a lot of issues that have nothing to do with making money and generating cash. The next thing you know, a competitor comes along and knocks you out of the box. Suddenly, your company doesn't have much of a future, and you may not have a job.

A good bonus system can help you build a bootstrapping mentality into your organization. It does that by putting a great deal of emphasis on job security by reminding people what it takes to protect their jobs and by showing them how they can get more.

There is only one sure way to protect jobs, and that is to be ruthless about costs. But least-cost companies face an unpleasant choice. If you want to come in below your competitors, you can (1) pay your people less or (2) make your product faster. That's about it. No humane person enjoys making such a choice. Who wants to have a business that provides people with the lowest standard of living in the market or that forces them to work so fast it's unhealthy? Who wants a company that prevents people from taking care of their families and themselves, from leading a full and happy life? But what's the alternative if you're going to be competitive and stay in business?

A bonus system like ours offers a way around this dilemma. It allows the company to hold base salaries at a level that gives people a great deal of job security—that pretty much guarantees they'll have work so long as they do a decent job. But if they do a better-than-decent job, if they can figure out ways to improve, the company shares with them whatever additional money they generate by paying them bonuses. The more they generate, the bigger the bonuses. It's like getting a raise, maybe even a very substantial raise, over and above your regular salary, but in a way that doesn't jeopardize your future employment. We know we can survive the tough economic periods. We may not pay bonuses in tough times, but we'll keep going. We won't lose jobs.

In effect, we're creating a certain elasticity for the down times. We don't ever want to lay people off, and we don't want to cut wages, either. Most of the salary a working person earns goes to cover his or her fixed costs—mortgage, tuition, groceries, transportation expenses. If you're forced to cut back in those areas, your morale is going to tumble. I don't know of anything harder than having to cut basic living expenses. We want people to be able to count on a certain level of income, but we also want to give them the opportunity to earn more. And they will earn a lot more as long as the company is in good shape and they are performing up to their capabilities.

If Bonus Programs Are So Great, Why Do So Many of Them Fail?

Probably for a lot of reasons our bonus program failed in 1983. It was a total disaster. For one thing, most people didn't understand it. They weren't motivated by it. They didn't know what they could do to achieve the goals. Not only that, but we'd chosen the wrong goals. We wouldn't have had enough cash to cover the bonuses if people *had* hit the targets. When we realized our mistake, we killed the program immediately, midway through the year, and went back to the drawing boards. That experience taught us how *not* to set up a bonus program. We've learned a lot since then about developing one that really works. In the process, we've come up with a checklist of what you should do, and what you should avoid, when you create your own bonus plan.

Do's and Don'ts for Bonus Programs
Put Everybody in the Same Boat

Every employee should be part of the same bonus program, from the chief executive to the people who sweep the floors and answer the phones. Give everybody the same goals and a similar stake in the outcome. At SRC, we calculate bonuses as a percentage of regular compensation. Whenever a bonus is paid under Stop-Gooter, each of us gets a check for an amount representing a preset percentage of our annual pay (salary, or wages plus overtime).

We don't all get the same percentage, however. Under Stop-Gooter, most managers and professionals are eligible to earn bonuses totaling up to 18% of their annual pay. For everyone else, the maximum bonus is 13% of annual pay. The reason is simple: we want people to move ahead, to take more risks and shoulder additional responsibilities. If they do, it's important that they get rewarded. But, that said, we want everyone to go after the same goals and to be subject to the same rules.

That's because we want people to play together as a team, to pull in the same direction. It's easier to win that way. We don't want people or departments to compete against one another. We don't want to set up squads that try to beat one another. We certainly don't want to pit managers against workers, or vice versa. We want a compensation system that encourages people to understand one another's problems, that gets them to work things out. We want people to see how much we all depend on each other, regardless of where we stand in the company. At SRC, you win when everybody wins, when the company wins. I don't want a company-wide bonus program in which some people win and others lose. The only ones who lose should be our competitors.

The one exception to this rule is safety. You have to generate awareness of safety as an issue, because that's the only way to prevent accidents, and I don't have any problem doing that through internal competition. We don't include safety in our Stop-Gooter program. Instead, we run separate safety contests in which we divide the company into teams, deliberately mixing people across department lines. One year, for example, I was on a team with all the people whose last name started with S. The idea was to see which team could go the longest without an accident, and we offered $62,000 in prizes. By reducing accidents, we managed to bring down our annual workers' compensation premiums by $100,000. So the safety program wound up netting the company 38 cents on the dollar. It was a win for SRC, and a win for everyone at SRC because the savings helped us on our Stop-Gooter goals for the year. But our main purpose was to get people thinking about safety and to keep them from getting hurt.

Stick to Two or Three Goals—and Get Them from the Financials

Giving people a long list of goals is like not having any goals at all. Build your bonus program around two or, at most, three goals per year. More than that just gets too complicated. The important thing is to choose the right ones. I want goals that keep people focused on the fundamentals of business: making money and generating cash. I also want goals that educate people about the different aspects of the business, that teach people exactly what it takes to be successful, that provide an incentive to do the right things. Finally, I want goals that make the company stronger by eliminating our weaknesses. As it turns out, you can get all of that by choosing your goals from the financial statements.

We almost always base one of our annual goals on pretax profit margins to ensure people stay focused on making money. The other goal has varied from year to year, depending on what we've seen as our biggest vulnerability at the time. As a general rule, however, we make a point of taking the second goal off the balance sheet, to make sure people also pay attention to generating cash.

Now, a funny thing happens when you choose goals from the financial statements. For every one you pick, you get about five or six others at the same time. Suppose we decide to go after liquidity, which you can measure by looking at what accountants call the current ratio. It's calculated by adding up all of your current assets (i.e., those you expect to convert to cash within the next 12 months, such as inventory and receivables) and dividing by all of your current liabilities (i.e., those you have to pay within 12 months, such as short-term debts and payables.) The ideal current ratio can vary greatly from industry to industry, but you almost always want to have more current assets than current liabilities. A ratio of two to one is generally considered quite healthy.

Whenever you can quantify a goal, you can set targets. You can decide how big a bonus people will earn by improving the current ratio a specific amount. To hit that target they have to pay attention to a whole range of factors: inventory levels, shipping schedules, operating efficiency, collection of receivables, negotiated terms with customers, and on and on. In the process, people get interested in various aspects of the business. Suddenly everybody wants to know about receivables. We have staff meetings where our accountant talks about which customers pay and how fast they pay. And people are interested because if customers don't pay, we don't have the cash—the customers do. And we can't use that cash, say, to reduce our short-term debt. And if we don't pay down the debt, we don't hit the liquidity goal, and we don't get that bonus.

So the bonus game takes people down the money trail, and they see everything that happens when customers are slow in paying their bills. They get an education in business and numbers and the accounting system. They learn how it all fits together. And they accomplish several goals in the course of going after one.

Give People the Chance to Win Early and Often

A bonus program is first and foremost a tool for motivating people. If it doesn't motivate, it isn't working. And what gets people motivated? Winning. There's really nothing like winning to make you want to go back and try again to do even better the next time. Set up your bonus program so that you put people on a winning track from the outset and then make it possible for them to keep winning right through to the end of the year.

That's the whole logic behind our system of payouts. After we choose a goal, we set the levels at which we will pay bonuses. There may be as many as five payout levels for each goal. With the profit goal, for example, the company's baseline is usually a pretax margin of 5%, while our top target is 8.6%. If we come in with a pretax profit margin below 5%, we don't earn any bonuses. If it's between 5 and 5.5%, we get into the first payout level, which pays hourly people bonuses equal to 1.3% of their regular pay. We hit the second level at a pretax margin of 5.6%, and the bonus rises to 2.6%. The third level starts at the 6.6% margin and pays 3.9% of regular pay. So it goes until the company gets to an 8.6% margin or better, at which point an hourly employee earns a maximum payout on the profit goal of 6.5%.

Coming up with the specific targets and payout levels is largely a matter of arithmetic. The numbers will, of course, be different for each company. You *must* do the math. The bonus system won't work if the math doesn't work. In making your calculations, however, do not lose sight of the fundamental purpose, namely, to get and keep your people motivated. Following are some general rules to bear in mind.

Set the baseline at the lowest point that still guarantees the company's security. Everybody must understand that the basic health of the company is paramount. Nobody should earn a bonus for doing the minimum required to protect jobs. We figure, for example, that a pretax profit margin of 5% is the lowest we can have without getting into trouble. (Remember, 40% of profits go to taxes, so that leaves us with about a 3% after-tax margin, which we need for working capital—replacing worn-out machines, handling swings in inventory, and so on.) On the other hand, you don't want to put the baseline so high that people get discouraged right off the bat. Keep the first payout level well within their range. At SRC, everybody knows we are capable of getting into the first level on either goal, because we set the baseline at a level we've already achieved in the past.

Notice that people are focusing *above* the survival point. Many companies set their goals too low, as if it's okay to break even. Then the company is in danger if people miss the goal. We never want to operate that close to the line. If our pretax margin is less than 5%, we all feel as though we've let one another down, and that's exactly how I want it. I would rather have people feel bad about missing the bonus than about losing their jobs because the company is not making money.

Make sure people have the opportunity to take home a significant portion of the additional profits generated under the bonus plan. Bonuses won't motivate people if they think the company is being cheap or greedy, or if the rewards aren't commensurate with the effort they're being asked to put out. They must feel that the plan is both a fair deal and a way to earn some big bucks. Stop-Gooter gives a machinist on the shop floor a shot at getting an extra 13% on top of his or her base compensation—that's $2,600 for someone making $20,000 a year. As for the company, it gives back to people, in the form of bonuses, about half of the additional profits generated over and above the base of 5% pretax (assuming we hit the highest payout levels on both goals).

Make it possible for people to earn bonuses frequently enough to keep them involved in the Game. One of the most common mistakes companies make is to have just one bonus payout per year. Then they compound the mistake by not announcing how much people have earned until long after the year-end, and not actually paying it for several weeks beyond that. What happens is that people ignore the bonus program until the final quarter—if you're lucky. More likely, they pay no attention to it at all and regard whatever they get under it as a gift. That kind of bonus is not a reward; it's a bribe.

We set up the Stop-Gooter program so that people have a chance to earn a bonus every three months. That makes sense because of our overall approach to "the Great Game of Business." On the one hand, we want people to get used to a quarterly grading system: it's a time-tested way of evaluating companies, and it works. It fits in with the normal cycles of a business. It's a good short-term time frame. Moreover, the three-month period turns out to be pretty much ideal for the way we play the Game. The end of the quarter comes fast enough that we can keep people focused on it through our weekly meetings.

Not every bonus program should have quarterly payouts. Monthly bonuses might work better for some companies. I can also see having semiannual ones. Don't go longer than that, however, without at least locking in the money owed to people. Not only will the bonus lose its impact, but you may run into credibility problems, especially if the program is new. People are going to be skeptical when you lay out the bonus deal for them. They won't really believe it until they see the money in their hands. But once that happens, their attitude will change so fast it will take your breath away.

Start with a small bonus pool and let it grow as the year goes on, so that people have the opportunity and the incentive to meet all the goals—and earn the entire bonus—right up to the end. By "bonus pool" I mean the total amount of money available to be paid out in bonuses during any given period. I'm saying the pool should start small and grow from month to month or quarter to quarter. This is a very important point. If you are not careful, you might inadvertently build some subtle demotivators into your plan. Suppose you decide to give people the chance to earn 25% of the annual bonus in each quarter of the year, and they come up short in the first two quarters. That would take a lot of steam out of the program. People might well get demoralized and stop trying. Suppose, on the other hand, they simply had to achieve the goals at any point in order to earn the bonus for the entire year—and they got everything done by the middle of the third quarter. Chances are that the company would be headed for big trouble before the year was through.

We avoid these pitfalls by increasing the stakes as the year goes on and by rolling any unearned bonus from one quarter into the pot for the next quarter. Here's how it works: the bonus pool for the first quarter is 10% of the total for the year. For the second quarter, it's 20%; for the third quarter, it's 30%; for the fourth quarter, it's 40%. Let's say we hit half of our targets in the first quarter and thus earn half of the available bonus. That amounts to 5% (half of 10%) of the total bonus we are eligible to earn during the year. We get paid the 5% we've earned right away; the unearned 5% is rolled over into the second quarter pool. So now, in the second quarter, we are going after 25% of the annual bonus pool (the 20% share for the second quarter, plus the 5% share left over from the first quarter). Suppose we don't hit any of our targets in the second quarter. In that case, the entire 25% gets rolled into the third quarter, which means we are now shooting for 55% of the annual bonus (the 30% share from the third quarter, plus the 20% from the second, plus the 5% from the first). Even if we hit all of our highest targets in the third quarter, there is 40% of the bonus pool available to go after in the fourth quarter. If we don't hit any of our targets, we still have a chance to earn the rest of the annual bonus (95%) before the end of the year.

As a result, people stay in the game right up to the last whistle. We can win one quarter at a time, or we can pull it out on a Hail Mary pass in the final seconds. Like the man said, it ain't over 'til the fat lady sings—and, by then, we have another game ready to go.

Communicate, Communicate, Communicate

Above all, make sure people understand how the bonus program works and are kept up-to-date on how they're doing. Bad communication is the main reason most bonus systems fail. No matter how clever you have been, no matter how well you have chosen your goals, no matter how carefully you have designed your payout system, your program simply won't motivate people if they don't get it, if they can't follow what's happening, or if they think you're hiding something from them. Don't expect them to give you the benefit of the doubt. I guarantee that they will think you're manipulating the numbers if there is any doubt about the bonus formula, or if you lack a system for monitoring and checking the results.

Of course, if the bonus program makes sense, explaining it shouldn't be all that difficult. Start by teaching the teachers—that is, your managers, supervisors, and key employees. Develop a solid core of people who know what's going on and who can explain it to everyone else. It's a good idea to hold some meetings and produce some support materials (handouts, brochures, videos, whatever). But once your teachers are up to speed, don't wait. Go ahead and launch the program. Most people are going to learn about the bonus game the way people have always learned about games: by playing it.

What's crucial is to have an effective system for keeping track of the results and communicating them throughout the company. Set a day and a time when the latest score will be announced each week (or, if that's not possible, each month) and then make sure you hit it. People will start looking forward to these updates. *Do not disappoint them.* If you are late with the scores, you will feed people's doubts and suspicions, dampen their enthusiasm, and undermine your chances of success.

How you communicate the results is up to you. Post them. Hold meetings. Put notices in with the paychecks. Set up an electronic ticker tape in the cafeteria and flash the score at lunch. If your people are spread out geographically, send the results out by fax or announce them by teleconference. Whatever you do, give people every opportunity to ask questions and get explanations. And go out of your way to make available the numbers on which the scores are based. Whether people actually check up on you or not, they want to know that they could if they had to. That's one reason for publishing complete, detailed financial statements every month. Ours run to a hundred pages, beginning with the monthly Stop-Gooter results. People could do their own calculations, if they were so inclined, from the numbers in the income statement and the balance sheet.

But keeping everybody up-to-date on the score is just part of the process required to make the bonus program work. In fact, the program should become the center of attention in your business. It should provide a context and a structure for everything else that goes on. If you've chosen the right goals, after all, achieving them should be everybody's top priority—by definition.

For the bonus program to play that role, there has to be a continuous, two-way flow of information between the people on the front lines and the managers who are overseeing the action. The top managers need numbers they can use to identify problems that should be solved, opportunities that should be pursued, victories that should be celebrated. The front-line people need constant updates on where they stand, and they have to be shown what they can do to improve the results. The middle managers need tools to motivate and to lead; to set priorities; and to draw the connection between meeting the standards, hitting the targets, and earning the bonus.

Obviously, we are talking about fundamental questions of management here. That's perhaps the most important benefit of a good bonus program. It provides a powerful incentive to make sure people throughout the organization have a clear understanding of their roles and the information required to perform them as well as possible. A company's ability to manage the flow of information will go a long way toward determining not only the effectiveness of its bonus program but also its ultimate success in the marketplace.

At SRC, we manage the flow of information by playing "the Great Game of Business." The principal mechanism we use is the weekly staff meeting, which is not so much a discrete event as the focal point for the entire process of exchanging information up and down the organization.

Don't Pay the Bonus Unless It Is Earned (But Do Everything You Can to Help People Win)

This is a simple point, but it is fundamental. The bonus program should be a tool for putting people in touch with the realities of the marketplace. A bonus should not be seen as a gift from management. It should be a reward people earn by doing a better job than their competitors who are out there vying for the same customers. You undermine that message if you pay the bonus when people come up short on their targets.

This can be very, very tough for a CEO. If people have tried hard and missed by a tiny amount, there is a big temptation to pay the bonus anyway. Resist it. Once you start changing the rules of the game, you step onto a slippery slope, and it is hard to go back. A couple of times, we have missed targets by .01%. In each case, it was agony. I never want it to happen again. So now, as we near the end of the quarter, our accountants come into the weekly meeting with sheets showing exactly what we must do to get to the next level on each goal. You can always come up with a few thousand dollars extra in some area, if that's what it takes.

Conclusion

The real power of the bonus program lies in its ability to educate people about business. Once they understand the math, they see how everything fits together, and how business can be a tool for getting them what they want. And it all does fit together. The system really works. You can't criticize it, because it is simply a reflection of reality. You can criticize individuals. You can take people to task for the way they do business. You can go after the ones who are greedy, who only want to help themselves, who exploit other people for personal gain. But the fault lies in those individuals, not in the nature of capitalism.

4

Equity Incentives in Entrepreneurial Growth Companies

Peggy Walkush

We know one thing for certain about today's business environment: the best, brightest, and most innovative and entrepreneurial people want a piece of the action—many won't even consider joining a company unless they receive stock. At a recent conference, Phil Bane, corporate counsel for First Virtual Holdings, commented that the technical staff members he is recruiting are "smart, savvy, have done research on the company, know the potential financial gains, and are poised to negotiate their equity stake."[1]

This attitude is so prevalent, particularly in companies employing "knowledge workers," that it prompted a major article titled "How to Get a Piece of the Action" in *Fast Company*, a new business magazine.[2] The article cites the example of Gordon Gould, a 27-year-old "information architect" who left a comfortable position at Sony Corporation to join a new media startup called Thinking Pictures, Inc., negotiating a salary increase and a 3.5% equity position in the process. "I'm young, but I'm not dumb," Gould explains in the article. "I know I'm a prime producer and I want my compensation to reflect that. If I'm going to spend 16 hours a day in an office, I want to be rewarded for the upside value my work generates. I want to feel that the company is partly my baby."

The reengineering and downsizing of major corporations over

the past 10 years has resulted in a wellspring of new companies, particularly in the high-technology and service sectors of the economy. The entrepreneurial movement is alive and well in America, as Ray Smilor, Vice President of the Center for Entrepreneurial Leadership in Kansas City, reported at a May 1996 breakfast workshop:

> We are in the greatest era of entrepreneurship in American history, maybe the greatest era worldwide. Last year, 750,000 new companies were incorporated in the United States alone. Since 1990, 600,000 companies have been incorporated in each and every year. That compares to 50,000 a year in the 1950s. There is also a proliferation of associations for entrepreneurs. . . . There's a push and a pull at work in our society. The push is that big companies are laying off, they're not creating jobs today. That's been well-documented since 1980. In fact, in the February 1996 issue of *Newsweek,* you will see pictures of CEOs of large corporations, and below them numbers—50,000; 60,000; 35,000. That's how many people they laid off that quarter. The pull is this proliferation of entrepreneurial activity, and it's remarkable.[3]

These emerging entrepreneurial companies have new and different ideas about building companies, which often translate into new ways of organizing people and compensating them for achieving goals.

The information in this paper is largely based on the practical experiences of the Foundation for Enterprise Development (F.E.D.) in working with entrepreneurial firms. Many of the companies that we at the F.E.D. work with are entrepreneurial growth firms—companies in the startup or early growth phase with less than 300 employees and projections for rapid growth over the next few years. Most are closely held, although some have plans to ramp up and take the company public in 4 to 6 years. Others plan to remain private, build the company, and later transition ownership to employees and/or management, or sell the company. All want to use equity incentives to recruit, retain, reward, and motivate employees.

My purpose here is to provide insight into the three main categories of questions asked in consultations with entrepreneurs and executives. They include (1) *tools of the trade:* what are the types of equity incentives and how do they stack up against one another?

(2) *industry trends:* what are other companies doing? and (3) *getting started:* how do you get started and what issues should be reviewed?

Because the companies we work with are typically looking to tie incentives to individual performance and offer stock to recruit, retain, and reward some, but not necessarily all employees, I will focus on stock methods that can accomplish these objectives—specifically stock options, stock bonuses, and stock purchase offers. I will not address plans that offer equity as part of a retirement benefit, such as employee stock ownership plans (ESOPs) and 401(k) plans, nor plans that require that all employees be allowed to participate, such as section 423 stock purchase plans, although these plans are important tools for providing broad-based employee ownership as a company grows.

Tools of the Trade

There are three primary methods for sharing stock with employees that offer great flexibility, including the ability to tie rewards to individual performance and allow owners and executives to offer different levels of stock awards to any and all employees. They are stock options, stock bonuses, and stock purchase offers.

Stock Options

Stock options give an employee the right to purchase a number of shares of stock at some time in the future, typically at today's price. For example, an employee may be granted the option to purchase 1,000 shares of stock at today's fair market value of $1 per share. The option grant specifies an expiration date, which means the employee must exercise the option by purchasing the shares before that date or forfeit the options. Options typically vest (i.e., become exercisable) over a period of time, which means the employee must stay with the company or meet specific performance objectives before receiving the right to purchase those shares. For example, if the 1,000 shares noted above vest over four years at 25% per year, then the employee could only exercise and purchase

250 shares after one year, another 250 after two years, and so on. In this example, if the employee were to exercise the options in total after four years, when the stock price has risen to $5 a share, the employee would purchase 1,000 shares for $1,000 ($1 per share), receiving shares now worth $5,000.

There are two types of stock options: incentive stock options (ISOs) and nonqualified stock options (NSOs). The differences between the two primarily have to do with the tax treatment to the company and the recipient. If the option in the above example were an NSO, the employee typically would have to pay ordinary income tax at the time of exercise on the $4,000 gain in the value of the shares ($5,000 current fair market value minus the $1,000 exercise price). The company would receive a tax deduction for the $4,000. Then, when the employee sold the shares in the future, let us suppose for $8,000, he or she would pay capital gains tax on the $3,000 difference between the sale price and the $5,000 value of the shares at exercise. In the case of ISOs, the employee in the above example would generally not pay tax until he or she sold the stock, at which time the entire gain of $7,000 (sale price of $8,000 minus the exercise price of $1,000) would be taxed as a capital gain. The company never receives a tax deduction in the case of an ISO.

In order to receive the positive tax treatment (for employees) of an ISO, many requirements must be met, including:

- Only employees may receive ISOs.
- The employee must hold the shares for at least two years after the grant date and one year after the exercise date.
- Shareholders must approve a written plan specifying the number of shares that may be issued and the class of employees that is eligible for option grants.
- The option cannot be priced at less than 100% of fair market value (110% for owners of 10% or more of the company).
- The grant value of options that may be exercised for the first time in one year is limited to $100,000 per person.

• The option term may not exceed 10 years (5 years for those owning 10% or more of the company).

Stock options are appealing to companies and employees for various reasons. First, stock options give employees a risk-free opportunity to share in the future success they help generate. Employees do not bear the risk of losing their investment because they do not have to purchase the shares until some time in the future, when the stock price has presumably increased. If the stock price falls below the grant price, an employee would not exercise the option. When priced at current fair market value, stock options do not dilute shareholder value because the options are only worth something (and therefore exercised) if the value of the company increases and thus all shareholders' value increases. Nonetheless, options are a precious commodity and should be used to leverage employee performance toward the goal of increased shareholder value. When used in excess, options arguably dilute shareholder value. For owners leery of sharing ownership too quickly, options can delay such sharing because employees do not become shareholders until they exercise the shares.

Another major benefit to the company is that stock options are free from an accounting perspective: the value of stock options does not have to be recognized on the books of the corporation, although it must be noted in a footnote to the financial statements. A compensation expense must be recorded when options are granted at a discount or when an option is classified as "variable," meaning that the number of shares or exercise price is not known or is contingent upon future events.

There are many levels of complexity that can be added to stock option plan design. The simplest and most common form is presented in the above example. NSOs can be offered at a discount to current fair market value, which is sometimes done to provide some immediate reward to the recipient, or they can be priced above fair market value when the intention is that the recipient benefit only if the stock price increases beyond some level, such as inflation or a minimum expected growth rate. Whenever a company sells stock to employees, securities laws (federal and state) must be carefully considered. While many exemptions exist, particularly in small companies with a limited number of highly paid employees purchasing stock and a limited amount of capital raised through purchases, it is always wise to consult a securities attorney.

Stock Bonus

A stock bonus is an award of a number of shares of stock to an employee. A stock bonus may be offered in lieu of a cash bonus to save the company cash during its early stages. A restricted stock bonus requires an employee to stay with the company for a period of time or meet performance objectives before receiving the right to the value of the shares. Vesting is most often tied to years of service. An unrestricted stock bonus does not require that any conditions be met before gaining the full value of the award.

With an unrestricted stock bonus, the employee must pay taxes on the fair market value of the award at the time of grant. If the value of the stock bonus is substantial, this can present a cash flow problem for the employee. For this reason, many companies pay bonuses half in cash and half in stock so that the employee can use some of the cash to pay the taxes. The employer may withhold taxes from the employee's paychecks over the calendar year in which the bonus is awarded, which argues for awarding bonuses early in a calendar year. The company receives a tax deduction for the same amount on which the employee is taxed.

With a restricted stock bonus, the employee pays tax on the fair market value of the shares as they vest. Let us take the example of an employee who is awarded a restricted stock bonus of 100 shares (with a current fair market value of $1 per share) that vest equally over four years. After one year, 25 shares vest; let us suppose that the stock price is now $1.50 per share. The employee pays taxes on $37.50 worth of stock at this point (25 shares times $1.50). After the second year, another 25 shares vest, and now the stock price is $2. The employee pays taxes on $50 at this point (25 shares times $2). Successive years are treated in the same manner.

The employee can make what is called an Internal Revenue Code section 83(b) election, which would allow him or her to pay taxes at the time of grant on all 100 shares at the $1-per-share price. This election is wise when the stock is expected to appreciate rather rapidly and when the employee expects to stay with the company over the vesting period. If the employee leaves before fully vesting in the shares, he or she will not receive credit for the prepaid taxes on the forfeited shares. Again, the company receives a tax deduction at the same time and for the same amount on which the employee is taxed.

For accounting purposes, a company must record a compensation expense for the market value of the stock at grant. If the bonus is restricted, this amount is charged to earnings over the restriction period. If vesting is based on meeting performance goals rather than on years of service, the compensation expense is adjusted each year as the stock price changes until the award is fully vested.

Stock bonuses are immediately dilutive to existing shareholders and create new shareholders upon award, which is viewed as a positive for those looking to create real ownership and as a negative for those concerned about having employees as owners right out of the starting gate. Even when vesting schedules are attached to stock bonus awards, recipients gain full voting rights as well as rights to receive information about the company upon the grant.

Stock Purchase Offers

A stock purchase offer gives an employee the right to purchase a number of shares of stock at a given price. The company may make a loan to employees, allowing them to pay for the purchase over time. The company may also discount the purchase price or offer a matching stock bonus or option award to encourage stock purchases by employees.

Stock purchase offers are particularly attractive to startup companies with little value to their shares. It allows employees to purchase large amounts of stock at a low price without any of the tax complications of restricted stock bonuses or options. Vesting schedules may be attached to the purchased shares, giving the company the ability to repurchase the unvested shares at the price the employee paid if the employee leaves the company before the shares fully vest. Vesting is typically not tied to purchased shares except in early-stage companies where employees are able to purchase shares at a low price (often at pennies per share).

An employee must pay tax on any discount received in purchasing stock, and the company receives a corresponding tax deduction. For accounting purposes, the company must expense the value of any such discount.

Stock purchases are an important way of raising capital for early-stage companies, and many owners believe that employee investment in the company builds commitment. Stock purchases are not dilutive (unless discounted) because they generate capital that increases company value and can be used to build the company.

A Quick Look at How the Methods Compare

Table 4-1 compares from several aspects the methods discussed above.[4] Probably the most important aspect to consider is the psychological effect of these various methods and their ability to achieve the desired objectives with the desired group of employees.

Psychological impact of stock purchases. Many entrepreneurs comment that stock is more meaningful to employees when they put some of their hard-earned cash on the table to purchase it. There is a growing interest in stock purchases for this reason. Entrepreneurs who offer stock purchases often find that employee investors take an active interest in their company and are more likely to ask questions about financial performance. Stock purchases build commitment to the company on the part of the employees who become owners.

Psychological impact of stock bonus. A stock bonus is like a gift of stock, and to me communicates that it is a reward for a job well

Table 4-1. Comparison Summary of Equity Sharing Methods

	Primary Advantage	Primary Concern	Psychological Impact	Tax Impact	Accounting Impact
Stock Purchase	Gain employee buy-in and commitment	Securities registration may be required	Powerful when employees invest their own funds	Typically none for employee or company	Typically none
Stock Bonus (Restricted)	Provides cashless reward tied to company performance	Tax impact to employee	Valuable reward for employee performance	Employee taxed as bonus vests; company gets corresponding deduction	Company must expense over vesting period
Stock Bonus (Unrestricted)	Provides cashless reward tied to company performance	Tax impact to employee	Valuable reward for employee performance	Employee taxed at full value at grant; company gets corresponding deduction	Company must expense full value at grant
Stock Options (NSO)	Limited value dilution since options only exercised if company value increases	Difficult for employee to understand	Gives employees a stake in future success they generate	Employee taxed at exercise; company gets corresponding deduction	No expense required, only footnote disclosure
Stock Option (ISO)	Limited value dilution since options only exercised if company value increases	Difficult for employee to understand	Gives employees a stake in future success they generate	Employee not taxed until sale as capital gain; company does not get deduction	No expense required, only footnote disclosure

done. In most cases, it is an "after-the-performance" reward. Restricting a stock bonus through vesting can make it a powerful retention tool. Some refer to unvested stock awards as "glue" or "golden handcuffs" that tie the employee to the company. One criticism of stock bonuses is that they are not as meaningful as stock purchases because employees do not have to pay anything for them. Unlike options, stock bonuses create real ownership on the day they are granted.

Psychological impact of stock options. Stock options, because of the tax and accounting benefits to the employee and employer, are probably the most widely used equity incentive in entrepreneurial growth companies. They are forward-looking: employees benefit only if company value increases and all shareholders benefit. Options say to employees, "work hard to make this company worth something in the future and you will be rewarded." For companies ramping up fast toward an initial public offering (IPO), stock options work well in providing employees with an incentive to make that IPO day a big payoff.

A major criticism of stock options is that they do not create real ownership. According to Matt Ward, CEO of WestWard Pay Strategies in San Francisco, the vast majority (over 90%) of employees in high-technology companies exercise and sell the same day, even when they hold ISOs, which would convert ordinary income into capital gains if they were to hold the shares for one year after exercise. A stock plan administrator in the Silicon Valley commented to me during a recent phone conversation that there is almost a fever among employees there that causes them to jump ship once a company goes public and they have cashed in their options, so they can join a new startup, gain options, and work toward the next big payday. So options clearly are a forward-looking, pay-for-performance tool that keeps people focused on the future, but whether they create employee ownership and build long-term commitment in public companies is questionable.

In companies planning to stay closely held, because they can decide when and how many shares to repurchase, this same mindset does not exist, especially where senior management has communicated to employees that the company does not plan to go public.

Industry Trends

One of the most common questions asked by entrepreneurs is "What are other companies like mine doing?" Too often, companies are looking for a cookbook formula. Unfortunately, cookbook formulas are hard to come by, and even if a competitor were to share his or her equity compensation scheme, it would not necessarily be the best approach for your company. As with any form of compensation, equity incentives must be designed with a company's unique issues in mind to complement its culture, mission, vision, and values. Nevertheless, it is useful for companies to consider survey data as a baseline to understand what industry trends prevail. Following are highlights from recent compensation surveys by Watson Wyatt, Coopers & Lybrand, and Hewitt Associates.

Taking Stock of High-Tech, Watson Wyatt (1995)[5]

The survey group consisted of 85 high-technology companies, of which 67 were public and 18 private. The survey covered the use of stock options. Annual ongoing stock option grants by salary level were as follows:

Base salary (in thousands)	Grant value as a percentage of base salary
Over $250	283%
$200–$250	115%
$150–$199	103%
$110–$149	77%
$90–$109	50%
$75–$89	32%
$60–$74	25%
$50–$59	25%
$40–$49	20%
$30–$39	14%
Under $30	8%

Annual total employee option grants (as a percentage of total options received by each group) were as follows:

	Non-officers	*Officers*
All companies	70%	30%
Revenues under $100 million	67%	33%
Revenues from $100 to $499 million	73%	27%
Revenues of $500 million or more	84%	16%
Private companies	46%	54%

The study also made the following findings:

• The median amount of total options outstanding, expressed as a percentage of total common shares outstanding, was 15.47%.

• The vesting schedules for options were as follows: four years (48.8% of companies); five years (25.6%); three years (15.9%); other (9.7%).

Total Compensation in Newly Public Hi-Tech Companies, Coopers & Lybrand (1996)[6]

The survey group consisted of 32 high-tech companies with recent IPOs (75% went public in 1994 or 1995, all since 1990). Data were gathered from proxies and prospectuses. Revenues ranged from a low of $389,000 to a high of $107 million, with an average of $24.2 million. All of the companies offered high-tech products and services, primarily telecommunications, Internet access services, and software applications.

The average percentage of ownership by position (displayed in terms of number of shares and options as a percentage of total shares outstanding) was as follows:

		Founders vs. non-founders
CEO	21.8%	32.6% vs. 13.4%
CFO	13.9%	12.4% vs. 2.0%
VP Technology	4.4%	9.6% vs. 2.4%
COO	13.9%	(not available)
Top Sales & Marketing	2.4%	(not available)
VP-Operations	1.3%	(not available)

The study also made the following findings:

- 84% of the companies have plans that allow for granting incentive stock options and nonqualified stock options.

- 25% of the companies grant restricted stock bonuses.

- 19% of the companies have an employee stock purchase plan (i.e., a section 423 plan).

- 16% of the companies grant stock appreciation rights.

- 85% have vesting periods between three and five years, with four years being most common.

On Employee Stock Ownership, Hewitt Associates LLC (1996)[7]

The survey group consisted of 55 companies with average sales of $6.8 billion and median sales of $3.0 billion. The industry breakdown was: 53% manufacturing; 11% retail; 9% banking, finance, insurance; 7% energy; 4% utility; 16% other non-manufacturing. The type of program(s) offered and the percentage of companies offering them were as follows:

> Stock options (67%)
> ESOP/401(k) mandatory allocation (35%)
> Stock purchase offers (24%)
> Restricted stock bonus (20%)
> Qualified "section 423" stock purchase plan (18%)
> Nonrestricted stock bonus award (9%)

The study also made the following findings:

- 65% of the companies offering stock options reported that fewer than one-third of their entire employee populations were eligible for stock options. The median was 15% of employees being eligible and an average of 36% of employees being eligible.

- The median number of option shares outstanding and set aside for future grants represented 6.5% of total shares outstanding.

- 91% of the companies offering stock options reported using a three-year vesting schedule.

Summary

It is difficult to compare findings among these three surveys because of the differences among survey groups and the questions asked, but they do provide some interesting findings. For example, the Coopers & Lybrand survey shows the equity positions of the key executives at the time of the public offering. Clearly the Coopers survey shows, and our experience has shown, that founders are able to negotiate a substantially bigger equity stake than a senior executive who is brought in several years after startup.

The Watson Wyatt survey shows data regarding option awards as a percent of salary. The option award is determined by multiplying the option grant price by the number of shares awarded. As would be expected, the award levels as a percent of salary ramp down pretty quickly below the $100,000-per-year salary level. Yet the survey also shows that most options are granted to non-officers. The companies in this survey were primarily public companies.

The Hewitt Associates survey was conducted on very large companies. It is interesting to note that 65% of these companies offer stock options to less than one-third of their work forces. It appears that these larger companies typically reserve equity incentives for top management. Is it any wonder that middle managers and technical professionals of larger companies are looking to join entrepreneurial companies and "get a piece of the action"?

Getting Started with Equity Sharing

The most critical step in designing an effective equity incentive program is to first define the company's strategic objectives for equity sharing. This typically starts in the form of questions entrepreneurs and executives ask themselves—questions such as "How can I . . ."

- Attract employees to my company whom I can't afford to hire, but who are critical to future growth and success?

- Reward employees who deliver high performance?
- Get all employees thinking and acting like owners?
- Motivate my core staff so they will work nights and weekends with me to make my business worth something?

After specific objectives are defined, it is important to consider who will receive equity incentives. This question can launch philosophical arguments about whether or not all employees should be included, but the bottom line is that most companies have a limited amount of equity incentives to offer, and, based on how and to whom they offer them, the financial and economic outcomes will differ. It is a complex puzzle with no one correct answer.

Short-term objectives clearly should drive equity compensation plan design, but it is also important to take into consideration the long-term strategy of the company and the role employee stock ownership is intended to play over time. Future liquidity plans, whether through an IPO, sale, merger, or internal market, need to be addressed. It is critical to consider short-term strategic needs in light of big-picture goals and real-world issues.

Most of the companies we work with plan to offer stock ownership opportunities to all employees at some point, although they usually differentiate between stock grants to all employees and grants to key managers and technical professionals. The thinking of many founders and CEOs addresses equity incentives on three levels:

1. *"I have several key executives who can make or break the company. I want to tie them in with equity incentives such that if they stay with the company over a period of time and help us achieve or beat our growth and revenue targets, they will be well rewarded."* These companies typically use vesting schedules on annual stock awards so that if the executive leaves, he or she will be walking away from substantial unvested rewards; they may want the executive to invest money in the company or put part of his or her existing compensation or bonus at risk; and

they often want rewards tied to individual performance goals or company revenue/profit targets. In addition, they may offer restricted stock or options in recruiting key staff members.

2. *"I want to reward outstanding managers and professional/technical staff members—those who are really contributing to our success—with equity incentives."* They often make discretionary stock awards, typically stock options or a restricted stock bonus, to people they and other managers recognize as key contributors.

3. *"I want all employees to have the opportunity to become owners."* They typically want all employees to be able to purchase stock, perhaps at a discount, or they may want to offer a small stock bonus award to give all employees an ownership interest.

Using Performance-Based Incentives to Meet Objectives

Following are a few examples of how equity incentives can be designed to meet different objectives.

Retain employees critical to success. Vesting tied to annual stock awards, whether in the form of stock options or stock bonuses, is particularly powerful in retaining employees. At any point, an employee may have several years worth of stock awards with some portion unvested, which may make him or her think twice before accepting an employment offer from another company.

Provide incentives for meeting specific business objectives. Preset agreements that state specific performance objectives and the level of stock incentives for achieving each can motivate employees to focus on goals important to the organization. Stock bonus shares or stock options, without vesting restrictions, are typically used in these agreements. A stock bonus or option award that vests based on meeting specific performance objectives can also meet this goal.

Offer equity together with lower-than-market salaries. Equity may be offered to supplement lower-than-market salaries when recruiting and retaining employees. In this case, an unrestricted stock bonus or restricted stock bonus may be used to give employees an equity stake and the potential to capitalize on the future success of the company.

Reward top performers. Stock bonus, stock option, and stock purchase offers can be used individually or in combination to reward performance, build employee commitment, and retain top performers. A restricted stock bonus rewards employees with an equity stake while providing an incentive for staying with the company and working hard. A stock purchase offer with matching stock bonus shares or stock options enables employees to demonstrate their commitment by investing in the company while providing an additional reward for current performance.

Build commitment through employee investment in the company. Stock purchases can be encouraged by offering employees discounts on the stock purchase price, by matching purchase offers with stock bonus or stock option shares, or by offering employees a loan that may be repaid through payroll withholding.

Determining Who Gets What

Company executives are always looking for guidelines for determining how much equity is enough (or the right amount). Industry surveys provide a baseline of data, but let's face it—motivating individuals is an individual matter. Executives should prepare projections for company value growth several years into the future, perhaps showing "projected," "best-case," and "worst-case" scenarios. These projections should take into account an estimated number of new shares to be issued to employees over this time period as well as account for anticipated rounds of capital. Projections should also be made for individual employee stock account values over time. This is critical in evaluating whether the planned level of equity incentives will be substantial enough to be meaningful to employees. Forecasting value will help determine how much of the company to share and how many employees to include in the program.

Determining Stock Price in Private Companies

To prepare projections of future value, a company must have a mechanism for determining company value and stock price. While ESOPs and other qualified plans require private companies to have an independent valuation to determine stock price, this is not required with stock bonus, stock purchase, or stock option plans. The procedure for determining the stock price should be spelled out in plan agreements. For private companies that are fairly small, a formula approach for determining value is the simplest and least costly to adopt.

A formula can be as simple as book value (however, one cannot use book value for ISOs) or can be more complicated and include elements such as projected earnings, fully diluted shares outstanding, and the cost to exercise vested options. Another simple approach is to use a multiple of earnings. Rules of thumb for determining appropriate multiples for different industries are available through compensation consultants and valuation firms and by looking at comparable public companies. Executives uncomfortable with devising a valuation formula may want to work with an independent valuation firm to develop an appropriate formula for their company. As a company's stock transactions involve greater numbers of employees and become substantial in value, hiring an independent appraiser may become prudent from a liability perspective.

Creating Liquidity in Private Companies

While a company has no legal obligation to provide liquidity for shares obtained through the methods described here, most people would argue that there exists a moral obligation to convert paper into cash within some reasonable period. It is reasonable to communicate that the company is offering equity incentives and will not be able to provide liquidity for several years as it ramps up and stabilizes. Most employees are willing to be patient as long as they see a glimmer of light (i.e., cash) at the end of the tunnel. In companies where the leadership has no foreseeable plan to allow employees to cash out some or all of their stockholdings, stock ownership is often viewed as worthless.

In addition to the commonly known methods of liquidity—an IPO, sale, merger, or leveraged buyout—there are other approaches to providing liquidity. The simplest involves reserving a portion of cash flow for stock repurchases. The company can ask interested employees to submit a request for stock repurchases on an annual or quarterly basis, and then prorate the repurchases based on the amount of cash the company has available. Another simple way to create liquidity is to informally match buyers and sellers. Internal markets run the gamut from an administrative assistant collecting names of interested buyers and sellers to the full-blown, Securities and Exchange Commission (SEC)-registered broker-dealer of Science Applications International Corporation. A securities attorney should be consulted before a company facilitates such trades.

Most closely held companies fear that if they make the offer to repurchase shares, all of their employees will rush to sell. In fact, experience shows that employees tend to hold their shares when they feel optimistic about the company's future, are treated like owners, and know that there will be another opportunity for them to sell some shares in the near future. In this situation, the employees who tend to sell shares do so because they need the cash to buy a home or send a child to college. The ability to sell some stock to meet these needs makes ownership even more powerful.

Concerns About Equity Sharing

There are several concerns shared by many owners and executives considering equity sharing. They relate to dilution, control, and minority shareholder rights.

Dilution. It is important for owners to distinguish the difference between percentage dilution (i.e., by issuing additional shares to employees, an owner's percent of the company decreases) versus economic dilution (i.e., an owner suffers economic dilution if the total value of his or her shares decreases). Most private company owners desire to maintain majority ownership control and to enjoy a rising value of their shares while sharing minority ownership with employees to achieve growth and productivity goals.

Entrepreneurs receiving venture capital rarely are able to maintain majority ownership of the company and typically end up with a minority stake along the lines of the findings of the Coopers & Lybrand survey discussed above.

The ownership percentage and economic dilution can be managed by projecting company value and additional shares issued into the future and by tying the issuance of new shares to company performance goals. Stock options protect against *economic* dilution to some extent because shares will be purchased only if the value of the stock increases.

Control. Some entrepreneurs and executives fear that by sharing ownership with employees, they are relinquishing their ability to run the company and make operational decisions without involving employees. Minority shareholders do not have the legal right to be involved in operational decisions.

However, employee shareholders do have certain rights relating to the voting of their shares and information sharing by the corporation. When employees receive ownership through direct stock methods such as stock options (after exercise), bonuses, or purchases, they gain the right to vote their shares on all matters that require a shareholder vote, including the election of the board of directors and the sale or merger of the company. Companies concerned with the voting and other rights of minority shareholders may consider issuing nonvoting shares, bearing in mind that anything that dilutes ownership rights most likely will also dilute the motivational effect of ownership.

The amount of information minority shareholders have the right to receive depends on whether the company's stock is registered with the SEC or the state. If the shares are registered with the SEC, the company must periodically disclose financial information, including audited financial statements; general information about the company's products, services, or customers; and compensation information on the top five officers. Complying with these disclosure requirements can be time-consuming and expensive. If the company is private, the laws of the state of incorporation determine what must be provided to minority shareholders. Many states do not give minority shareholders the right to receive general financial information or salary information, but you should check the rules of the state(s) in which you are issuing shares.

Stock restrictions. One way to control who owns a corporation is through stock restrictions. While a corporation cannot put absolute control on who can own its shares, it can place restrictions on the shares to keep them out of the hands of competitors or other individuals who may have interests adverse to the corporation. The most common stock restrictions among private companies are the *right of first refusal* and the *right of repurchase at termination.* The right of first refusal gives the company the right, but not the obligation, to match any offer made to purchase the company's shares. The right of repurchase at termination gives the company the right, but not the obligation, to repurchase the shares of a terminating employee.

Minority shareholder rights. Majority owners owe a "duty of fairness" to minority shareholders not to waste corporate assets. This does not mean that a majority shareholder must seek the opinion of minority shareholders before making strategic investments. Wasting of corporate assets comes into play when, for example, a majority owner pays himself a salary that is seven times the industry average and unjustifiably so. Most challenges by employees who are minority shareholders relate to the undervaluation of their equity holdings paid out upon termination. For this reason, it is wise to have the method for determining stock price spelled out in the shareholder's agreement that employees sign.

The Journey of Equity Sharing

Equity sharing is a journey, not a destination. It is an ongoing process. It evolves along with a company's leadership, ownership structure, and strategic objectives. It plays different roles at different points in a company's life. Equity incentives often look very different in the startup phase than in the fast growth phase; in the pre-IPO phase than in the post-IPO, public company phase; and in the young, private company phase than in the mature, post-leveraged buyout phase.

It is impossible to overemphasize the importance of employee communications and involvement in getting employees to think and act like owners. Regardless of its form, for stock ownership to be meaningful to employees, employees need *information*—about the plan, their work environment, company performance and goals; they need *knowledge*—about how the business runs, about the company's critical numbers, about owning stock, and about how their performance affects stock price; they need *participation*—opportunities to be heard and to help solve problems; and they need *power*—decision-making authority where their work is concerned, autonomy, and responsibility.

In conclusion, employee stock ownership works best when the following characteristics are present:

- The leader articulates a clear vision for sharing equity.
- Equity sharing is designed to logically (and fairly) support the company goals and culture.
- Emphasis is placed on communications—about the company, the stock plan, the company's vision and mission, and the corporate culture.
- Liquidity is provided within a reasonable time frame.
- Employees are treated like owners by being given responsibility, autonomy, and opportunities to offer feedback and ideas.
- Equity participation is meaningful, not token.
- All employees are given the opportunity to own stock.
- The company is committed to growth.

Equity incentives, when designed to be an integral part of a company's culture and reward system, are a powerful tool for reaching the hearts and minds of employees. The challenge lies in creatively structuring equity incentives to have the greatest desired effect on every employee.

Notes

1. Remarks at the F.E.D.'s eighth annual "Building the High-Performance Company" conference, San Diego, California, September 27, 1996.

2. See Eric Matson, "How to Get a Piece of the Action," *Fast Company*, October/November 1996.

3. Remarks by Ray Smilor, Vice President of the Center for Entrepreneurial Leadership, at the F.E.D. Breakfast Workshop, "Leadership in an Entrepreneurial Company," San Diego, California, May 6, 1996.

4. This table was developed by the F.E.D. for the CD-ROM "Building Your Company: Using Equity to Encourage High Performance," produced by the Center for Entrepreneurial Leadership of the Ewing Marion Kauffman Foundation in Kansas City.

5. *Taking Stock of High-Tech: Stock Options in the High-Technology Industry* (Watson Wyatt Worldwide, 1995).

6. *Total Compensation in Newly Public Hi-Tech Companies* (New York: Coopers & Lybrand LLP Survey/Research Unit, 1996).

7. *On Employee Stock Ownership* (Hewitt Associates, 1996).

Chapter

5

Performance-Based Stock Options

Arthur S. Meyers

This chapter explores the legal, tax, and accounting considerations of performance-based stock options. A brief review of the consequences of issuing stock options may be useful, particularly for the reader who lacks significant experience with equity compensation programs.

For tax purposes, options are divided into two principal categories: (1) incentive stock options (ISOs) and (2) nonqualified stock options (NSOs). Employee stock purchase plans (including tax-qualified "Section 423 plans") are not covered by this chapter.

An ISO is designed to provide an eligible employee with capital gains treatment on the amount of both the spread at exercise and any gain upon sale if the stock is held for at least two years from the date of grant and one year from the date of exercise. (The "spread" is the difference between the fair market value of a share of stock subject to the option on the date of exercise and the exercise price.) The option holder must be employed by the issuer (or a parent or subsidiary) at all times from the date of grant of the option until the day three months before exercise.

The exercise of an ISO may result in Alternative Minimum Tax [AMT] liability to the employee. Various factors, including the amount of the spread, the amount of itemized personal deductions, and the employee's martial status, affect the AMT calculations.

If an employee sells or otherwise transfers the ISO shares before satisfying the holding requirements or without satisfying the ISO's employment requirement, the employee will be deemed to have engaged in a "disqualifying disposition," and the ISO will receive the same tax treatment as a NSO (described below).

While ISOs can produce very favorable tax consequences for employees, the tax consequences are not favorable from an employer's tax perspective in that an employer does not receive any deduction upon the exercise or the qualifying disposition of shares by the employee. Employers issue ISOs because they may be demanded by executives (particularly lateral hires), the business is not generating a profit (and so will not miss the deduction), or the company expects the employee to dispose of the shares prematurely (which will result in a tax deduction for the company).

With an NSO, the option holder (who may be an employee, director, or consultant) is taxed at exercise on the difference between the fair market value of the purchased shares at the date of exercise and the exercise price. This spread is treated as ordinary income and is subject to taxation as if such amounts were wages. The company receives a corresponding deduction if it reports the income to the Internal Revenue Service (IRS). The amount of the spread is treated as wages for FICA purposes. Any gain on the sale of the shares over the option holder's basis (the spread plus the consideration paid by the option holder) is treated as a capital gain.

The accounting treatment of an option will not vary by its status as an ISO or NSO under federal income tax rules. Instead, the relevant inquiry is whether the stock option is subject to "fixed" plan accounting or "variable" plan accounting as described below. (For purposes of this chapter, it is assumed that the issuer has not elected to comply with Financial Accounting Standard 123, *Accounting for Stock-Based Compensation,* for financial accounting purposes other than with respect to the mandatory pro forma footnote disclosure of the effect of the fair value of stock option grants upon net income and earnings per share. It is further assumed that the plan pursuant to which the options are granted is not intended to be treated as a capital-raising program or "non-compensatory" plan, as would be the case with most Section 423 or employee stock purchase plans.)

Accounting Principles Board Opinion No. 25, *Accounting for Stock Issued to Employees,* (APB 25) prescribes the general principles for accounting for stock issued to employees. It provides that the compensation cost of compensatory stock plans is to be measured at the "measurement date"—the first date on which both the number of shares and the exercise price are known. Under some option plans, the number of shares and the exercise price are known at the date of grant. When the measurement date occurs on the date of grant, the plan is treated as a "fixed" plan for accounting purposes because the compensation cost (usually zero) is determinable and not subsequently adjusted. Most stock option plans are designed to be fixed plans.

If the measurement date occurs after the date of the grant (either because the number of shares or the exercise price is not known at the date of grant), then the company must record the estimated compensation cost for each accounting period over the remaining vesting period until the measurement date occurs. At that time, the final compensation cost is determinable. Such plans are known as "variable" plans because the compensation cost varies each accounting period until the measurement date. For example, assume that a company issues an option to purchase 4,000 shares of company stock at the end of a four-year period, with an exercise price equal to the fair market value as of the date of grant but subject to the company's revenues growing by 50% or more. For each of the four years, the company's financial statements would reflect an estimated compensation cost for the options. To calculate that cost each year, the company would multiply the number of shares (here, 4,000) by the difference between the fair market value of the shares as of the end of that year and the fair market value of the shares as of date of grant. That product would then be multiplied by the percentage of the vesting period (25%, 50%, 75%, or 100%) which had elapsed as of the end of the year for which the calculation is being made. Finally, the accrual for the year would be calculated by subtracting from that amount the cumulative amount, if any, of expenses charged for any prior years of the option vesting period. This procedure is also known as "marking to market." The actual expense would not be known until the end of year four, when it could be determined whether or not company revenues grew by 50% or more.

As of this writing, the Financial Accounting Standards Board (FASB) is considering a proposal that would require companies to use variable plan accounting for any repriced option grants. Current industry practice generally allows at least two repricings of a grant before the grant would be subject to variable plan accounting. Under FASB's proposal, a company would be required to report the estimated compensation cost for each accounting period until the repriced option is exercised. The measurement date would not occur until the repriced option is exercised, as the company could conceivably change the exercise price again.

Overview of Performance-Based Option Plans

There are a variety of performance-based stock option plans. Most of the plans contemplate the issuance of NSOs. Some of the plans produce fixed accounting, while others produce variable accounting. In many instances, a company's board of directors will find it appropriate to adopt a performance-based option plan even though the program will constitute a variable plan and will result in a charge to earnings. These companies have made a determination that the corporation's goals may be more efficiently attained through a plan which produces variable accounting. Of course, not all performance-based options result in variable accounting.

Set forth below is a brief description of the most common performance-based option programs. In practice, these techniques generally are not used for broad-based stock options. Performance-based option plans are not applied below the senior executive level for several practical reasons. Performance-based plans often result in variable plan accounting. Companies would likely incur significant charges to earnings if they were to extend an option plan that produces variable plan accounting to many individuals. Also, it is unlikely that any individual in a nonexecutive position could influence the company's stock price significantly through his or her own efforts. Additionally, the adoption of a compensation plan that sets dozens or hundreds of individually tailored performance targets could prove administratively unwieldy.

Performance Grants

Under a performance grant arrangement, a company grants stock options to an individual if certain company, subsidiary, division, or individual performance targets are met. Both the decision of whether to grant any options and the size of the option grant are based upon performance. The options could be immediately exercisable or may be subject to further time vesting. In some instances, the options are issued at a discount, although the company would be required to recognize a corresponding compensation cost. Performance grants produce favorable fixed plan accounting, but should be viewed more as a bonus plan than an option plan because they reward past accomplishments.

Performance-Accelerated Options ("Time-Accelerated Options")

The issuance of performance-accelerated options is very common. (These options are also sometimes referred to as "time-accelerated options.") Under this arrangement, options are granted with a normal vesting schedule. The options are typically granted at a price equal to the fair market value of the company's shares at the time of issuance so as not to result in any compensation cost to the company. The options vest with the passage of time in accordance with a normal vesting schedule (e.g., 25% after the first anniversary, and monthly thereafter at the rate of 25% per year). If, however, the stated performance goals are met, vesting is accelerated. Common performance goals include the attainment of a certain share price for a number of consecutive days (e.g., for 10 out of 20 consecutive trading days) or the attainment of other company (e.g., EBITDA—earnings before interest, taxes, depreciation, and amortization) or individual (e.g., sales) goals. Performance-accelerated options are normally accorded fixed plan accounting treatment. Although performance-accelerated options constitute an improvement from a shareholder's perspective over regular time-based vesting of options, they do not eliminate eventual vesting. Attempts have been made to use 10-year vesting schedules with accelerated vesting for performance. Care must be taken not to trigger variable plan accounting in light of comments by Securities and Exchange Commission (SEC) representatives on the limits of when such arrangements would continue to be accorded fixed plan accounting by the SEC. Generally, the SEC is willing to recognize performance-accelerated options as fixed plans if the options are granted using a vesting schedule no longer than the vesting schedule the company normally uses, the vesting schedule does not exceed eight years, and the vesting schedule is not more than two or two-and-one-half times the performance vesting period.

Premium-Priced Options

Premium-priced options are issued in the same fashion as traditional stock options, except that the strike price is significantly higher than the fair market value of a share on the date of grant. For example, if a company's shares are currently trading at $10 per share, an executive might be granted an option to purchase a number of shares at $15 per share. In order to obtain an economic benefit from such options, the market price of a share of stock must rise after vesting to a level above the exercise price. If the company's stock does not reach the premium exercise price within the term of the option (usually only a few years), the option would be expected to expire unexercised. Under such arrangements, however, the option holder must have the right to exercise the option when it vests, even if the fair market value of a share of stock is substantially below the exercise price, in order to be accorded fixed plan accounting treatment.

The pricing aspect of these options can provide "political cover" for mega-grants to executives. On the other hand, many programs require huge and fast runups in a company's stock price to generate large gains. Monsanto Company (before its announced merger with American Home Products Corporation) and Transamerica Corporation are examples of companies that maintain premium-priced option plans. Under more recent versions of premium-priced option programs (such as Monsanto's), executives are being asked to invest a portion of base salary or bonus to purchase premium-priced options and to retain a substantial portion of the net shares after exercise.

Premium-priced options raise interesting estate and gift tax possibilities. Under a recent revenue ruling (Rev. Rul. 98-21), the IRS took the enforcement position that transfers of options are not treated as completed gifts for gift tax purposes until the options are vested. If a company is willing to issue a significant number of transferable premium-priced options on an immediate vesting basis, an executive may find it very attractive to transfer these options to family members as the value of a premium-priced option for gift tax purposes would be much lower than the value of a market-priced option.

Price-Vested Options

Price-vested options are also known as target price options or performance-contingent options. Under a price-vested option, an executive is granted options to purchase shares at the fair market value of the shares at the date of issuance. If the stock reaches a certain price by a stated date, then the executive vests in the options granted. Otherwise, the option is forfeited. Thus, performance is a condition of vesting.

Price-vested options are often granted in tranches. For example, a price-vested option issued when a company's shares trade at $40 each may provide that one-fourth of the options will vest when the stock price hits $48 per share, another fourth when the price hits $52 per share, and the balance at $60 per share. In some cases, particularly where the premium is 50% or higher and the option term is five years or less, the options are issued with an exercise price substantially below the then-fair market value of the company stock in order to enhance the acceptability of such arrangements to executives. A discounted purchase price might be as low as 50% of the estimated Black-Scholes present value of the vesting price.

On its face, a price-vested option may appear to be similar to a premium-priced option. The two are quite different, however. With a premium-priced option, an executive is encouraged to cause the company's stock price to rise to a specified level and is then rewarded by sharing in stock price gains above that level. With a price-vested option, the executive is given the same instruction, but is rewarded with the full appreciation on each option share from the date of grant if the target share price is reached. Also, a premium-priced option program is treated as a fixed plan, while a price-vested program is treated as a variable plan for accounting purposes. Citicorp adopted such a price-vested option plan before its merger with Travelers Group.

Performance-Vested Options

Performance-vested options attempt to link the vesting of options (and therefore the compensation payable under such arrangements) to the attainment of specific performance goals of the company or the executive rather than just stock price increases. Otherwise, performance-vested options are very similar to price-vested options. For example, a company may issue options with a strike price equal to the fair market value of a share of company stock determined as of date of grant and provide that the options do not vest until the company attains a 20% rate of return on shareholders' equity over a specified period. Another example of a performance goal would be the requirement that the rate of return to shareholders is at least equal to the 75th percentile peer group shareholder return. Performance-vested option plans could also provide for vesting if earnings per share increase a specific amount per year for several years, if cash flow increases at stated rates, or if revenues increase beyond normal projections. Some programs may require the attainment of multiple company performance goals. Bank of America is one example of a company that has granted performance-vested options.

Options may also be structured to provide for vesting only if individual performance goals within the executive's control (e.g., divisional sales) are met. Performance-vested options keyed to such factors allow the executive to focus on internal factors that promote the long-term health of the company. In all such cases, if the performance goal is not reached, the option is forfeited.

Indexed Options

Under an indexed option plan, a set number of options are issued, but the exercise price is not known at the time of grant. Rather, the exercise price increases beyond the share price at the date of grant each year (or other performance period) based upon an external index. A variety of indexes could be used. A company could link the exercise price to a stock market index, such as the S&P 500 or the Russell 2000. Or it could tie the exercise price to the stock prices of an industry peer group. Alternatively, a board of directors could decide to increase the exercise price by a treasury bond rate index in order to reward executives for returns beyond what shareholders would receive in a nearly risk-free investment.

From the shareholder's perspective, indexed options reward executives only for outperforming the industry peer group or other index. Average performance or general stock price appreciation would not increase executive compensation. For example, if a company issues an indexed option at $30 per share and the index rises 50% by the time the option is exercised, the exercise price of the option will increase to $45 per share.

Unfortunately, indexed options result in variable plan accounting and therefore charges to earnings. Indexed options may also reward executives in a declining stock market. For example, if a company falters, but it still performs better than its peer group, the executive stands to profit because the indexed exercise price falls faster than the company's stock price. This latter shortcoming can be handled through proper plan drafting, which would not permit the exercise price to fall below fair market value at date of grant. Few public companies have adopted these programs to date. One such company is Level 3 Communications.

Full-Value Grants

In addition to issuing performance-based options as described above, some companies grant shares outright (subject to certain restrictions or conditions) or require their executives to purchase shares in order to more closely link executive compensation to the performance of the company. The thinking here is that it is not appropriate for the executive to benefit from the upside of stock ownership with none of the downside risk assumed by stockholders. There is also much less dilution to existing stockholders when shares are purchased or granted rather than when options are issued.

Restricted stock is increasingly being used to take advantage of the lower capital gains tax rates enacted as part of the Taxpayer Relief Act of 1997. The exercise of stock options (which are typically NSOs) produces ordinary income that is taxed as high as 39.6%. If an executive is granted restricted stock and makes a Section 83(b) election at the time of grant to recognize as ordinary income the value of the shares, then all appreciation from the date of grant will be taxed at the 20% capital gains rate. Of course, the executive is taking a risk that the he or she will remain employed for the duration of any time-based vesting schedule and that the shares will appreciate from the date of grant. For executives at certain companies, this risk is modest. Accordingly, some companies have added performance features to restricted stock.

In some cases, companies have chosen to accelerate the ordinary vesting of restricted stock if the company performs well. These programs are known as "TARSAPs" (time-accelerated restricted stock award plans) or sometimes "PARSAPs" (performance-accelerated restricted stock award plans). TARSAPs allow performance criteria to accelerate the lapse of the vesting restriction without affecting the ultimate award; they thus produce fixed plan accounting.

In other instances, companies grant "performance shares" under which vesting is contingent upon stock performance. Typically, a percentage of the stock award vests each year as certain appreciation levels are reached and sustained for a number of consecutive trading days. Performance-shares require variable plan accounting, with the ultimate charge to earnings being the appreciated price of the stock at vesting. Boeing is one of several companies that have adopted such a performance share plan.

Performance shares have an advantage over performance-based options in that the same gain can be generated for executives with fewer shares, which results in less stockholder dilution. Many full-value grant programs also enable the recipient to receive company stock dividends.

Conclusion

When implementing a performance-based stock option program, a company must also consider other equity compensation concerns, such as the satisfaction of the performance-based exception to the $1 million limitation on compensation of senior public company executives under Section 162(m) of the Code, any prohibitions to the use of the arrangement under state corporate law (such as the use of indexed options where the option price could fall below the fair market value of the company's stock), the proper treatment of the options under federal securities laws (the manner of proxy disclosure and status as a derivative security for purposes of Section 16 reporting), and the impact upon the company and the executive in the event of a change in control under Section 280(G) of the Code. With respect to the latter point, which is beyond the scope of this chapter, it should be noted that the acceleration of performance-based options upon a change in control will produce less money for an executive who is subject to the typical 280(G) cap on compensation in an employment agreement or a stock option agreement than would be the case for comparable options issued with time-based vesting.

Of course, the most significant consideration is whether the plan results in variable plan accounting and therefore charges to earnings. The use of performance-accelerated options is widespread. The use of premium-priced options is growing. Both of those types of option programs are treated as fixed plans. To the extent that the FASB, under its Repairs and Maintenance Project for APB 25, produces more circumstances under which variable plan accounting may occur and institutional shareholders continue to clamor for greater linkage of pay to performance, there may be increased acceptance of variable plan accounting for senior executives and therefore greater usage of price-vested, performance-vested, and indexed option programs in the future.

Simulating Employee Ownership with a Rolling Bonus Program

Corey Rosen

For many very small businesses (typically those with two to ten people), and for some larger ones, it is impractical to set up a plan that actually shares stock with employees. There are a number of possible reasons for this. The company may be a partnership, sole proprietorship, or limited liability company (a kind of hybrid partnership/S corporation) and thus not have any stock to share. For S or C corporations, sharing stock is a possibility, but not necessarily a desirable one. The legal costs of setting up an ESOP (employee stock ownership plan) will almost always be prohibitive ($20,000 or more in most cases). A 401(k) plan in which the company contributes shares to employee accounts is unappealing in an S corporation because the plan would have to pay "unrelated business income tax" on its attributed share of corporate earnings. That tax could often be at the highest personal tax rate. Presumably, the company would have to make additional contributions to the plan to pay the tax (otherwise, the plan trustee would be imprudent to accept company stock as a contribution). A 401(k) plan with employer stock as a matching contribution from the company may make sense for a C corporation, although it would be necessary to have the shares valued each year to protect against potential employee lawsuits and IRS claims for improper deductions.

Some companies will consider selling stock to employees, but this requires them to purchase shares with after-tax dollars and may require costly financial disclosure statements. Giving stock to employees can avoid these securities issues, but the gift would be taxable to the employee at the time of receipt, even though the employee may not be able to sell the shares for some time into the future.

Stock options may make sense for S or C corporations, but raise potentially difficult issues. First, the company must provide a way employees can turn the shares they buy with their options into actual cash. Most companies offering options broadly envision being sold or going public to make this possible. Otherwise, companies must buy the shares back themselves or arrange a market among employees. This may be difficult to do in smaller companies. Salaries are typically lower, and employees may not, as a result, have as much discretionary income to buy out another owner with after-tax savings as would be the case with executives of larger organizations. Small companies are also less likely to have either the cash flow or access to credit that larger companies have to make a redemption possible. Second, when employees start exercising their options, companies must comply with at least the anti-fraud disclosure requirements of state and federal securities laws. The required statements to employees usually cost $15,000 or more to prepare and require detailed financial information to be shared. Finally, in some companies, explaining the complexities and uncertainties of stock options (how they work, how a price for options is determined, how they are treated from a tax standpoint, and so on) can be daunting.

Aside from all these practical considerations, some business owners are simply not comfortable with the idea of sharing actual ownership, usually because they fear a loss of control or potential future litigation from unhappy shareholders. Nonetheless, they want to provide an incentive for employees that is linked not to short-term profits or some limited measure of performance, such as sales increases or quality control, but instead to the growth of the company over an extended period of time. This article describes an approach that can accomplish this objective in a way that imposes the least risk and entails the lowest costs for both the employer and the employee.

Phantom Stock: Not as Good as It Seems

For many small company owners, phantom stock often seems like the perfect solution to the equity sharing puzzle. In practice, however, phantom stock plans usually raise too many problems to be used as a means of providing equity to most or all of a company's employees. In a phantom stock plan, employees would be given a payment in cash at the end of a designated period of time equal to what would be the value of a designated number of shares. For instance, an employee might be given 100 shares of phantom stock in Quantum Mechanics, a small automobile diagnostic shop. At the time of the gift, Quantum had 1,000 total shares outstanding. These shares would be assigned a value at the time of the award, usually by the board of directors. The value would commonly be based on book value or some formula related to earnings or cash flow (these formulas usually produce a value that is considerably different from what a more thorough and professional appraisal would produce). No actual shares would be transferred. At some point in the future, usually when the employee leaves, he or she would receive the current value of those 100 shares. That value would be affected by the growth of the company and by how many additional shares the company has issued over the ensuing years. Each time new shares are issued, the ownership interests of other owners is diluted, unless the value of the phantom shares is recalibrated. Properly structured, the employee should not have to pay tax at the time the phantom shares are awarded. When the cash payment is made later, it will be taxed as ordinary compensation and will be tax-deductible to the company. If the company has no shares, employees can instead be given a phantom percentage of the total company equity.

This sounds like the perfect solution, but it raises many difficulties. First, if the company actually puts money aside to pay for the phantom stock, it cannot take a tax deduction for these funds. Moreover, if the funds accumulate to a large enough amount, the company could be subject to an excess retained earnings tax. If the company does not set aside the money, employees may, with reason, not have much faith that they will ever actually get anything from this plan. Second, if the plan provides for phantom shares for most employees, the U.S. Department of Labor may claim that it is actually a retirement plan in disguise and must be subjected to the expensive regulations of retirement plans—but without any of the accompanying tax benefits. Phantom stock is not appealing from an accounting standpoint either; the company must accrue a charge against earnings for the accrued liability in its outstanding phantom stock units. Finally, the very name "phantom" can make getting employees enthused a difficult task. For all these reasons, phantom plans are almost always recommended only for a limited number of key people in a company.

The Rolling Equity Bonus: A Simple Ownership Equivalent

By varying the phantom stock idea somewhat, we can create a system that should function smoothly. It would work much like a stock appreciation rights plan (SAR), except that, unlike most SARs, it is specifically designed to make an annual payout, it is based on equity performance over a short period of time, and it is not tied to providing employees cash to make an actual purchase of shares. The idea is to mimic what would happen if employees were given stock options. With a stock option, an employee has the right to buy a certain number of shares at a price fixed today for some number of years into the future. When the option is exercised and the shares are sold, the employee ends up with the spread between the grant price and exercise price. If the option were granted at $10 in 1998 and exercised and sold at $18 in 2003, the employee would get $8 net for each share. In the best-designed option plans, employees get new options each year, thus giving them an ongoing interest in the company. While some old options will be exercised at various times, employees will always have new ones to give them an interest in the company's future.

With the rolling equity plan, an employee instead gets a bonus to be paid at some future point based on the increase in the company's equity value. Each year, employees are given a promise for an additional bonus at a point further into the future. Because employees are not given an irrevocable right to a future benefit (their right to get paid in the future is subject the "significant risk of forfeiture" that they may not still be employed when the bonus is paid), the payout should be accounted for as a compensation cost only when it is paid out. At that point, it would be treated like any other wages or bonuses.

An illustration makes this concept clearer. Instead of issuing stock, in 1998, Quantum Mechanics tells employees they will get a bonus in 2001 based on a percentage of the increase in the equity value of the company. This can be based on a book measure or a formula, such as one based on a price-to-earnings ratio. In 1999, for instance, Quantum would announce that in 2002, there will be another bonus if the equity value in 2002 exceeds the equity value in 2001 by a defined amount. This approach can continue in three-year increments every year. The bonus would be treated as compensation to employees in the year paid and would be deductible to the company at that time.

There are a number of variations on this theme, of course. For instance, a company could apply a vesting concept so that employees would only get the bonus in any year if they had been working for the company for the three prior years. The number of years could be varied, and the bonus need not be given annually. There could be a trigger for the bonus, such as reaching a stated profit, sales, or retained earnings target. Obviously, the percentage of the growth in equity that is distributed can be whatever the company chooses and can change from year to year. The way the bonus is allocated is also optional; it might be based on relative pay, for instance, or some merit judgment.

If the company is sold, employees can get a share of the sale proceeds, provided the plan is designed appropriately. To do this, the plan should state that should the company be sold, employees will get the same share of the increase in equity value that results from the sale as they would have earned if a three-year period had elapsed.

This system has a number of advantages. Unlike other ownership plans, it does not require employees to wait until they leave the company or some other far off event to get a reward. In large, well-established companies, this is less of an issue because people can see a long-term career path, know the company has a track record, and are more easily convinced that a promised benefit will be paid. In newer and smaller companies, employees may not identify with the company's long term goals and may be more skeptical of the value of owning shares in the company. In the rolling equity plan, employees can be given a realistic time horizon to be paid, but still have a clear interest in helping the company grow long term.

A second advantage is that it gives the company a context in which to explain to employees what the numbers for the business mean and what they can do to reach them. That, after all, is the point: getting employees to understand how to think and act like business people.

Finally, the system is infinitely flexible and legally simple. It is nothing more than a bonus program that has somewhat different parameters than the usual annual Christmas bonus. It can be designed and implemented with relatively simple special legal advice. It would be desirable, however, to have a financial advisor help think through how an equity measure can be built and how much of the increment employees should get.

As a company grows or, if not an S or C corporation, becomes one, it may reach a point where the advantages of a formal employee ownership plan become more important. Employees will already understand the basic concepts of equity sharing, so the transition to actual stock, along with the usually considerable tax advantages a formal plan brings to them, should make this transition a smooth one.

Designing Shorter-Term Cash Incentive Programs: Getting the Basics Right

Fred E. Whittlesey

Those interested in understanding stock-based compensation find themselves faced with a barrage of buzzwords describing various types of plans: stock options, employee stock ownership plans (ESOPs), employee stock purchase plans (ESPPs) . . . the list goes on. But the topic of incentive compensation, which rightly includes stock-based plans though it typically refers in practice to shorter-term cash-based programs, has its own vernacular: variable pay, lump sum awards, bonus, commission, gainsharing, profit sharing, and more. I have even seen this proliferation of terminology lead to debates over "risk sharing" versus "success sharing."

Compensation management comes down to this challenge: effective allocation of an organization's financial capital to its human capital. Every organization, whether for profit or not-for-profit, private sector or public sector, faces this challenge. In some manner and in some form—cash, stock, goods, and services—capital must be allocated to ensure people will accomplish the work of the organization.

Increasingly our human capital means more than employees; it includes other workers such as contractors, consultants, and other professional advisors, making it necessary to consider how we allocate capital to the organization's *workers*, not just its employees.

Developing an allocation plan requires determining who receives the capital, in what amount, based on what criteria, and then integrating this process with other management systems.

Employee ownership discussions typically revolve around the allocation of stock, but it is possible—indeed, sometimes preferable—to use cash-based programs to reinforce ownership processes, including information-sharing, empowerment, and participation. This chapter will help readers understand how to use shorter-term cash-based incentive compensation programs to reinforce ownership behaviors and create an ownership culture.

Allocating Capital: Stock-Based Plans

When we allocate financial capital to workers in the form of stock, some aspects of plan design are easy to resolve. While there are many accounting, tax, and securities law complexities, the performance measurement is usually predefined: stock price. Over time, total return to shareholders (stock price appreciation plus dividends) determines exactly how much compensation will be paid, linked directly to company performance. This inherently addresses three fundamental issues of reward strategy:

- *Performance measurement,* defined as total return to shareholders.

- *Economic consequences of performance:* in most plans, rewards are linear with increases in shareholder value.

- *Funding* provided by the marketplace (public or private) when the equity position is liquidated.

Many organizations, unable or unwilling to use actual equity for compensation, attempt to emulate a stock-based program through a long-term cash bonus plan, which often gets labeled as phantom stock or stock appreciation rights (SARs).[1] To manage an organization effectively, however, we need to focus on shorter-term measures, shorter-term behaviors, and shorter-term performance as well. We can choose stock or cash as the form of reward delivery. When we consider allocating cash or stock based on shorter-term performance (weekly, monthly, quarterly, but most commonly annually), we run into some difficult issues.

Performance Measurement

The first issue to resolve is performance measurement. If an organization embarks on an incentive compensation development process without knowing, in concept, the performance basis, the effort will be ineffective. Once we allocate stock to a worker, we know the ultimate value of that reward will be based on the stock price. The only other decisions are how many shares to allocate and what criteria will determine share allocation. But when we allocate cash it must be based on some behavior, as gauged by some measure or measures, over some period—and none of these has an inherent design answer.

For example, when the total quality management (TQM) movement began to spread widely in the early 1990s, many organizations modified their plans to reward quality, which led to failed programs and caused many to question the effectiveness of incentives. The unfortunate answer is that the wrong question was being asked. Quality is not the ultimate objective of an organization, but a strategy for meeting objectives. Clarifying objectives is the critical first step in defining performance measures as a basis for incentive compensation.

I have a simple analogy to illustrate the core issues of performance measurement (figure 7-1). Even for those who are not sports fans, this model clarifies the key issues in developing effective performance measures for shorter-term incentive programs. It contrasts the variety of performance measures in a typical business organization with those of a professional football team.

The *ultimate* objective of a for-profit entity is total shareholder return, not market share, worker satisfaction, or quality products, which are strategies. To link incentive compensation to performance measures, we must understand the types of measures are *critical* to achieving the organization's ultimate objectives. And there are many *interim* measures that contribute to higher-order measures.

The Hierarchy of Performance Objectives

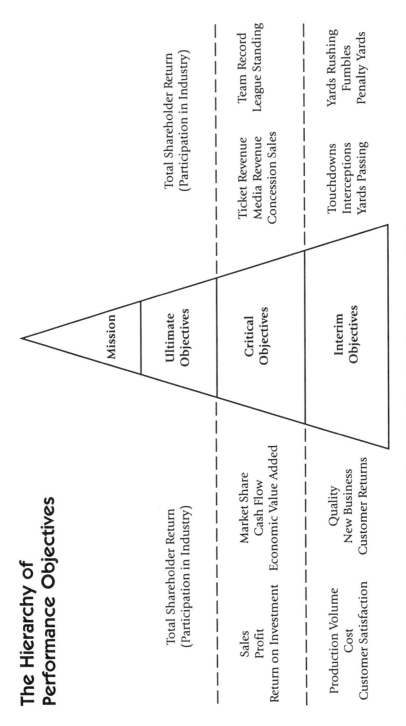

Figure 7-1. Hierarchy of performance objectives

Measuring Organizations and Individuals

The owners of any business, including a football team, have a dual agenda. Although they certainly want and expect a competitive return on investment, they typically direct their investment not only to a potentially profitable venture, but one in which they're interested. So they have two goals: shareholder return and industry participation. Owning a football team can be very profitable, but many wealthy investors choose instead to sponsor an auto racing team or invest in oil drilling operations to achieve their investment objectives.

But a football team owner would have little success in approaching the defensive linemen and telling them their job is to ensure a 25% return on the owner's investment. Imagine the blank stares. That is, in fact, their job, however. Sadly, this is no different than an electric utility that tells its linemen (who climb poles rather than tackle opponents) that compensation from their new stock option plan is based on increases in stock price, which depends on earnings per share (EPS) growth. In both cases, the shareholders are attempting to link rewards to the organization's ultimate objective: increasing shareholder value. And in both cases the worker is unlikely to understand how tackling quarterbacks or repairing power lines affects return on investment.

Clearly, certain measures will lead to increases in value if managed properly. But the variety and complexity of these factors may still be beyond many workers' lines of sight. The defensive tackle still may not see the connection between his performance and concession sales volume (although professional athletes are quickly catching on to the commercial appeal of their brand). But the defensive tackle's performance—continued thrashing of the other team's players—may be what generates the excitement that entices fans to attend or watch the game, thus increasing overall revenue.

When we talk about creating an ownership culture, that is really the focus. How do we get every worker to understand how he or she affects overall performance? How do we help flight attendants understand their impact on the company's stock price, then link compensation to their behaviors accordingly? We typically use stock as our currency when we pursue this strategy. But that doesn't have to be the case. Many companies are unwilling, or unable, to use stock as the primary currency for performance-based compensation, yet succeed in creating an ownership culture.

Regardless of company size, an environment where employees feel the impact of ownership economics—upside and downside—is possible without the use of equity. While this chapter will not explore the role of related processes such as information sharing and participative management, these strategies need not be any different for a quarterly revenue sharing plan than for a retirement-oriented ESOP or stock option plan with a four-year vesting schedule and ten-year term.

Designing effective shorter-term incentive programs requires understanding and clarifying the ultimate, critical, and interim objectives along with the responsibilities for achieving them, then tying them to significant economic consequences for workers.

Understanding Incentive Alternatives

Management compensation plans were the source of performance-based cash compensation, just as they were the origin of equity-based compensation. Generally, the higher a worker is in the management hierarchy, the more performance measures lean toward ultimate objectives; the lower in the hierarchy, the more focus on critical or interim objectives (figure 7-2). From a financial perspective, the question is where we draw the line on the income statement. Senior management is responsible for total return on capital and is directly involved in managing both return and capital. A sales manager may have responsibility only for revenue, perhaps gross margins.

When we extend this to all workers, we have the proliferation of buzzwords (figure 7-3) we've been subjected to over the years. Some have emerged recently while others date back to the early part of the century. These result from attempts to resolve the issues of performance measures and organization levels in developing performance-based reward programs. Organizations considering performance-based cash compensation should not be intimidated by this plethora of terms. My clients' experiences show

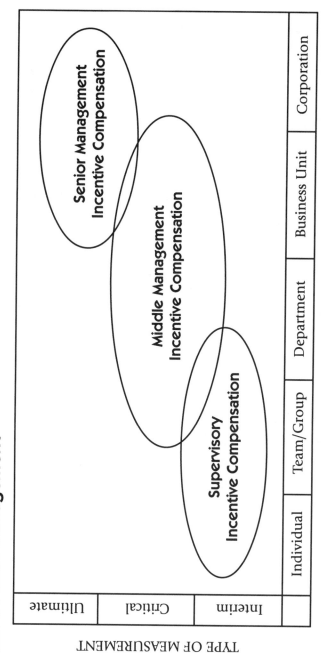

Taxonomy of Short-Term Incentive Plans: Management

Figure 7-2. Taxonomy of short-term incentives: management

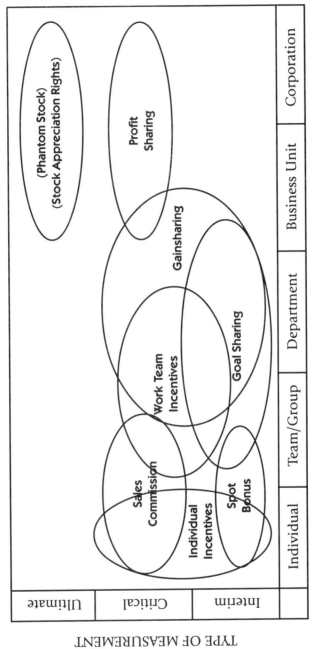

Figure 7-3. Taxonomy of short-term incentives: all workers

that a solid business-based process can lead through this maze of labels, and the final product—an effective performance-based reward program—can be named at the end. The key is understanding critical design decisions and the central issues of each.

Design Decisions

Many key design decisions in shorter-term cash-based incentive programs parallel those in the equity-based plan design process, not unlike the journalist's who, what, when, where, why, and how. But because we have more flexibility, the process requires more thought to arrive at the best answers, answers that address these components:

Participation. Who will participate in the plan? When we design an ESOP, there's little leeway. With a broad-based option plan, it is typically the same: all employees, maybe including nonemployee workers. The flexibility of shorter-term cash based programs allows a single program for everyone or just for some, or multiple programs including some or all employees. We need to determine whose behavior we are trying to change.

Performance Measures. Next, for that group or groups, what types of behavior do we seek and what outcomes do we want? What do we need them to do that they're not doing? What do we want them to stop doing? This requires defining the term *behavior* quite broadly. The first behavior a worker exhibits is responding to the company's need for workers, then interviewing, accepting the offer, and showing up the first day. The final behaviors are giving notice, winding down, leaving . . . and telling others about their employment experience after they leave.

Between the beginning and end are the behaviors we typically seek to change. But "performance" includes joining, staying, and leaving as well as actual contributions to productivity on the job. Hiring bonuses, retention bonuses, and severance packages are no less a part of shorter-term cash-based compensation strategies than profit sharing, gainsharing, and sales commissions.

Performance Measurement Level. At which level should we link performance? Corporate, business unit, division, department, work group, individual—or some combination? This is often a difficult decision as we attempt to balance line of sight with team orientation, and immediate impact versus long-term impact. The lower in the organization we go and the more we move from line to staff positions, the more difficult it is to resolve these questions. The chief financial officer should be tied primarily, if not exclusively, to company financial performance. But what about the controller? assistant controller? accounts receivable clerk? There is no easy answer to these issues, but the outcome must be consistent with all other organization philosophies and strategies. "We're all in this together" or "It's everyone for themselves." "I don't have control over that" or "We all have an impact on everything."

Performance Period. What is the relevant period for measuring performance? In most cases, a shorter-term cash incentive plan will have a performance period of one year or less. This convention in compensation design reflects the one-year horizon of the accounting cycle: annual financial statements, current versus noncurrent assets and liabilities, and so on.

We need to provide rewards on a cycle consistent with the organization's decision-result cycle, regardless of quarterly and annual fiscal periods. One company has sales representatives on a weekly commission plan—it sells advertising in a weekly publication, and the customer must decide each week whether to advertise again. Another company has technical people working on products with a two- to three-year development cycle and a two- to three-year market life. It pays milestone awards during development and a royalty-based award after the product is released. This decision will differ most by industry and company strategy and least by company philosophy.

Performance-Award Scale. How much pay for how much performance? If we have a simple percent-of-results formula—e.g., sales reps receive a straight commission of 5% of sales—this is self-defining. But relying on a simple linear formula may yield unexpected results. In fact, in my consulting experience this is one of the most common sources of compensation disasters.[2] More often, there is a business need to ensure a minimum performance level.

It is clear that we should be willing to pay our target incentive award at our target performance level. Below that, we must decide at what level we are no longer willing to pay. This defines the "performance threshold": the level where we consider the worker to have already been fully compensated for efforts and results through base salary, benefits, and other forms of reward.

Above the target level, we must determine when we are willing to pay 10% more, 20% more, 50% more, and so on. At what point, if any, would we be willing to double the award? Or are we willing to continue increasing the award proportionately as performance increases, with no cap? If the plan has multiple performance measures, this scale may vary among the measures. For example, an incentive compensation program with a revenue and operating margin matrix may have a threshold of 80% of target for sales and 70% for operating margin (table 7-1).

This decision drives the need to conduct detailed financial modeling of any proposed incentive program before implementation.

Funding. Where will the money come from? This critical decision defines not only the plan's financial operation but also the organization's reward philosophy. Some feel an incentive opportunity should be "self funding"—that is, incentive dollars become available only when performance exceeds an expected level; this is the basis for most gainsharing plans. Others believe the incentive is part of the total cash compensation budget paid for target performance; this is typical of most executive incentive and other target-based plans.

A formal funding formula may ensure a certain level of organization performance occurs before incentive awards are paid, as a control to ensure individual awards, in aggregate, do not exceed the organization's ability or willingness to pay. Alternatively, we can simply set individual award targets and, through detailed financial modeling, make sure individual and organization perfor-

Table 7-1. Example of a Revenue and Operating Margin Matrix for an Incentive Compensation Program

Operating Margin %	Margin Award Factor	Percentage of Targeted Award Paid				
13.0%	130%	65%	104%	130%	143%	156%
12.0%	120%	60%	96%	120%	132%	144%
11.0%	110%	55%	88%	110%	121%	132%
10.0%	100%	50%	80%	**100%**	110%	120%
9.0%	90%	45%	72%	90%	99%	108%
8.0%	70%	35%	56%	70%	77%	84%
7.0%	50%	25%	40%	50%	55%	60%

Award Factor	**50%**	**80%**	**100%**	**110%**	**120%**

Revenue (in Millions)	$160	$180	$200	$220	$240
Percentage of Target	80%	90%	**Target**	110%	120%

mance levels, as defined in the plan, are well-integrated with the award structure. This is often not the case, however, and aggregate individual awards may end up above target while overall company performance is below target. This is more of a performance management issue than a compensation design issue and beyond the scope of this chapter, but it supports the need for thorough analysis of a plan's financial dynamics before implementation.

The funding method must be considered along with the performance-award scale. There may be no separate formula, or a formula may be based on a threshold, target, and maximum (table 7-2).

Allocation to Individuals. How do we determine the amount of payments to individual workers? Several alternatives are available for determining the amount. Most plans establish a target percentage of base salary and a percentage-of-salary performance-award scale, often combined with multiple performance objectives. But many still use a percentage of profit, an equal percentage of pay

Table 7-2. Sample Funding Formula

Return on Invested Capital	Percentage of Target Incentive Pool Funded
18%	130%
17%	120%
16%	110%
15%	**100%**
14%	90%
13%	70%
12%	50%
below 12%	0%

to all workers, or an equal dollar payment to all workers (usually only in unionized environments).

Award Payment. Once earned, when should the payment be made? Most shorter-term incentive programs pay awards soon after the performance period ends. This ensures a reasonably short period between performance and reward. The lag between performance completion and reward is typically extended only to collect and confirm the information on performance. For an annual plan, this may require completing the audited financial statements.

Regulatory Considerations

Addressing the above issues results in a blueprint for an effective shorter-term incentive program that holds all the potential of equity-based programs for creating an ownership culture. Before implementation, however, we must consider certain regulatory factors. Shorter-term cash programs are subject to substantially less regulation than stock-based programs, but several issues may render a conceptually effective plan design administratively or legally prohibitive:

- *Overtime Calculations.* The Fair Labor Standards Act and many state labor laws require inclusion of lump-sum incentive award payments in the base rate for calculating overtime.

- *Benefit Calculations.* Companies implementing new add-on plans should review all existing benefit programs to verify the definition of "compensation" and determine whether the current plan includes, or should include, incentive awards in the calculation. This may affect life and disability coverage, defined benefit and defined contribution plans, and other plans with pay-related formulas.

- *Securities Regulations.* Most cash-based incentive compensation plans with performance periods of one year or less will not be subject to securities regulations. But federal and state securities regulators are now moving toward characterizing any compensation plan based on company value as a security and are imposing certain reporting requirements.

- *ERISA.* The Employee Retirement Income Security Act of 1974, as amended, prescribes rules for any plan that may be characterized as a retirement plan. In practice, deferring payment of earned awards beyond the termination date or for more than two years may subject the plan to ERISA reporting requirements and even funding requirements.

Implementing and Integrating the New Plan

A new incentive program must be designed with the organization's current total economic reward system in mind. The reported failure of many incentive programs can be attributed to implementing a plan with an insignificant reward opportunity relative to the existing reward structure. Employers should remember that the current group of employees has come to work for the company for, presumably, an acceptable total compensation and employment structure. An added form of compensation, if expected to change behavior, must bear some relative and absolute measure of magnitude to existing rewards.

For example, a new incentive program that offers a target award of 3% of base salary is likely providing a 1% to 2% potential increase in total compensation. When compared, in the worker's mind, to the potential for a 3% merit increase, a 2% sick day bonus (five paid sick days per year), and other explicit and implicit rewards, a behavioral change is unlikely to occur. A more significant shift in total compensation may be necessary, e.g., freezing base salary for three years while adding 5% per year to the incentive pool, resulting in a more significant reward opportunity: 15% of base salary, which is then 10% below market average. This highlights the need for both "gain" and "pain" in a true ownership environment.

The first plan described above is considered an "add-on plan," where a company already offering a comprehensive compensation and benefits program offers to pay additional compensation. The latter is termed a "replacement plan," where a new incentive plan substitutes for some or all of an existing form of compensation. While a replacement plan is often perceived as more controversial and requires more intensive communication, it produces more significant and rapid changes in behavior.

Joining the Performance Revolution

The *Wall Street Journal* recently reported that in 1997, for the first time, the majority of US employees participated in a performance-based incentive compensation program having some portion of pay at risk beyond the stale "merit increase" in base salary. Although the *Journal* did not explain the criteria for this assessment, I know of no organization not already using or considering performance-based cash compensation for every employee. This is occurring in publicly traded companies, closely held companies, government entities, nonprofit organizations, and companies worldwide as capitalism spreads.

U.S. employers have spent decades experimenting with incentive compensation, with much written about the successes and failures. As with any management technique, many good ideas are implemented in the wrong environment or with little thought to the details, yielding failure. But it is hard to argue with the long-term success of the U.S. economy, which is based on a combination of cash and equity-based return directly related to economic performance. The economic system works, and capital is allocated among organizations to its most efficient use. The same system works just as well *within* an organization, but must receive at least a fraction of the thought and effort that has led to our nation's success. We will then be able to allocate the organization's financial capital to its human capital in a way that ensures economic success for all parties.

Notes

1.   Fred E. Whittlesey, "Expanding the Phantom Stock Concept," *Compensation and Benefits Review*, November–December 1994.

2.   Fred E. Whittlesey and Carol L. Maurer, "Ten Common Compensation Mistakes," *Compensation and Benefits Review*, July–August 1993.

Chapter 8

Gainsharing and the Scanlon Plan

Paul W. Davis

Today there is increased interest in gainsharing, a management concept that has endured for over half a century. Gainsharing is a guiding management philosophy of at least 5 of the "100 Best Companies to Work for in America": Herman Miller, Donnelly, Beth Israel Hospital, Motorola, and Dana all credit at least part of their world-class performance to their gainsharing systems.[1] A comprehensive study conducted by the American Compensation Association beginning in 1991 and published in 1994 found that companies averaged over $2,410 per employee per year in productivity and quality improvements after installing gainsharing. After deducting program expenses and paying bonuses on average of $867 per employee per year, gainsharing provided a 134% return.[2] The financial results are impressive, yet they are only one of the many benefits of gainsharing. Study after study has found that gainsharing also improves employee involvement, communication, teamwork, labor relations, and quality.[3]

The renewed interest in such an old concept can be attributed to pressures that organizations are now facing. As they downsize, they seek ways to motivate the remaining employees. As they become flatter, the old methods of compensation (number of direct reports, etc.) are no longer effective. As competitive pressures increase, they seek ways to increase productivity and quality. After adopting Total Quality Management (TQM) practices, they seek ways to reward and coordinate teams. Unable to afford the high cost of adversarial relationships and ever-increasing base wages, union and management leaders look to gainsharing as a way to encourage cooperation within collective bargaining.

What Is Gainsharing?

The Japanese have a fable about a crow and a cormorant. In this ancient tale, a crow admires the cormorant, a black water bird that can swim to catch fish. The crow reasons that because he is a black bird like the cormorant, he too should be able to swim, so he dives into the water, only to drown. The fable's lesson is that things that appear to be the same may not, due to subtle, unapparent differences. Those interested in gainsharing should remember the crow's experience, because gainsharing systems that at first appear to be identical reveal fundamental differences upon closer scrutiny.

Gainsharing is a generic term with widely different definitions. For many, gainsharing is simply a group bonus calculation. For others, gainsharing describes a very sophisticated organizational development strategy. For the purpose of this chapter, gainsharing will describe any organizational process designed to increase productivity, quality, and financial performance by sharing "rewards" with groups of employees. Furthermore, in this chapter gainsharing will refer to practices that include (1) establishing specific goals, targets, or baselines; (2) communicating these goals, targets, or baselines to a group of employees; and (3) sharing rewards when the goals, targets, or baselines are exceeded.

This operational definition of gainsharing will not include discretionary management "bonus" practices such as an annual Christmas bonus because they are not tied to the specific performance of the company. In addition, it will not include individual piecework systems because they reward individuals and not groups. However, profit sharing will be considered a form of "gainsharing."

The ABCs of Gainsharing

Most of what is written about gainsharing concerns the mechanics of bonus formulas because various gainsharing systems are typically classified by how the bonus formula is constructed. In these articles, Scanlon Plans, Multicost Scanlon Plans, Rucker Plans®, Improshare®, Profit Sharing, etc., are reduced to a paragraph that only an accountant could love. While the formula is important for gainsharing success, it is only one factor among many that differentiate the various approaches. Recent research indicates that bonus formulas may not be the most important factors in gainsharing success.[4] Furthermore, almost all articles written since the 1960s about the Scanlon Plan's bonus calculation are misleading in documenting Scanlon evolution. They have not kept up with current Scanlon theory or application. While they are valuable as history, they provide little insight for those interested in the current state of the art in gainsharing.

The final reason why the formula approach to describing gainsharing is no longer effective is because it describes fewer and fewer gainsharing applications. Historically, gainsharing plans were one-size-fits-all packages, developed by consultants who trademarked their approaches. Improshare® and Rucker® are two of the most well known. While Improshare® Plans are still being installed, the Rucker® Plan did not survive long after the death of its creator. Today, there are still consultants trying to trademark their approaches, but most gainsharing systems are customized to the unique needs of each organization.

A new method of classifying the various gainsharing approaches is needed if the reader truly wants to understand the critical differences and make an informed choice. This chapter will attempt to help the reader understand the ABCs of gainsharing. This simple device, in which A stands for Assumptions, B for Business literacy, and C for Commitment, will help readers understand which gainsharing approach is right for them. If the ABCs can be mastered, the rest of gainsharing (including designing the bonus formula) will be easier. Because there are only two classic approaches that have survived the test of time, Scanlon and

Improshare®, they will be used to highlight differences in philosophy and application.

The "A" of the ABCs: Assumptions

All gainsharing systems are developed for some desired end. Typically, the motivation is to produce greater profits, to produce higher quality goods or services, or to encourage labor-management cooperation. At the heart of every gainsharing system are assumptions about human motivation and behavior at work. Gainsharing systems take on specific characteristics based on the assumptions of those that lead, design, and operate them. These assumptions define the program to a much greater extent than does the method of bonus calculation.

The "B" of the ABCs: Business Literacy

All gainsharing systems claim to increase productivity, profits, or performance. Some are based on the idea that the only thing needed to generate these improvements is more financial motivation, while others stress the importance of teaching employees about the business so that they will know what to improve and how to participate in improving it.

The "C" of the ABCs: Commitment

Gainsharing is a way to change the commitment level of people at work. All gainsharing systems attempt to shift commitment from the individual to a group or organization. The various approaches differ in the size of the group and the level of commitment they attempt to create.

Assumptions About Human Motivation

Throughout human history, we have sought to harness and control human motivation. We have used a wide range of "motivators" to get people to do what we want. We have used punishment from slavery to starvation, and we have used rewards from concubines to precious metals. As society became more civilized, we developed money as the universal form of exchange. With industrialization, we developed a wage system in which people work for money that they can then use to purchase desired goods and services. Despite thousands of years of experimentation, there is still great disagreement about what does and does not motivate. Because motivation is the primary reason organizations install gainsharing, the debate is not academic. Research has produced results that at times seem to contradict what most of us assume is common sense. For example, we have learned through research that money may not be as powerful a motivator as non-monetary rewards. Psychologists have attempted to unravel the mystery of human motivation, yet there are still wide differences of opinion on (1) whether one human being can motivate another—is motivation intrinsic or extrinsic? (2) what motivates people at work; (3) what the best way is for managers to motivate workers; and (4) whether money is the universal motivator.

Can One Human Being Motivate Another?

All gainsharing systems use some form of incentive or financial reward. So, like the crow in the Japanese parable above, we might assume that all gainsharing philosophies believe deeply in the power of extrinsic motivation. They do not. Scanlon Plans place more of an emphasis on the intrinsic motivation created by participation and education than on the extrinsic motivation created by money. Improshare® Plans place more of an emphasis on extrinsic motivation. Alfie Kohn, author of *Punished by Rewards: The Trouble with Gold Stars Incentive Plans, A's, Praise, and Other Bribes*, argues that the only thing accomplished when we try to motivate others is to destroy the intrinsic motivation in each of us. He quotes one of the foremost management scholars and researchers on human motivation, Frederick Herzberg, who wrote:

> Managers do not motivate employees by giving them higher wages, more benefits or new status symbols. Rather, employees are motivated by their

own inherent need to succeed at a challenging task. The manager's job then, is not to motivate people to get them to achieve; instead, the manager should provide opportunities for people to achieve so they will become motivated.[5]

Herzberg said this about the typical manager's common-sense approach to motivation:

> Managements have always looked at man as an animal to be manipulated with a carrot and a stick. They found that when a man hurts, he will move to avoid pain—and they say, "We're motivating the employees." Hell, you're not motivating them, you're moving them.[6]

What Motivates People at Work?

Researchers and management scholars believe that we each have different needs and, therefore, different motivators. Abraham Maslow stated that human beings fulfill their needs in a certain order. First, they have a need to eat, sleep, and breathe. He called these physiological needs. When these needs are met, he predicted, people would seek to have their security and safety needs met. Maslow believed physiological, security, and safety needs are lower-order needs. When these needs are met, people seek to have their social or affiliation needs met. Next they strive to have their esteem or ego needs met. When all the other needs are met, people seek self-actualization or self-fulfillment. Maslow believed social needs, esteem needs, and self-actualization needs are higher-order needs. Lower-order needs have more to do with our bodies; higher-order needs are related more to our minds.

Frederick Herzberg's work on motivation found that what motivates people is different from what turns them off. He found that working conditions, salary, benefits, status, and security were not motivators. He called them "hygiene factors" and realized they were similar to Maslow's lower-order needs. While they have the capacity to turn people off, they have little capacity to turn people on. Hygiene factors are a base from which the higher-order needs can be addressed. The "motivators" he discovered were responsibility, achievement, recognition, and satisfaction in the work itself. These, he realized, were related to Maslow's higher-order needs.

Herzberg's research indicates that if we want to motivate workers, we must first make sure that we have a base to work from. We must create security by driving out fear, providing insurance, and so forth. We must provide an adequate salary so the need for food and shelter can be met. Once this base is in place, we can help to provide "motivators" by creating organizations that allow the higher-order needs for affiliation, esteem, responsibility, recognition, and self fulfillment to be met.

Managers who accept Herzberg's research would create as part of any gainsharing approach opportunities for employees to have their social needs met (perhaps by having them work in teams). They would design their gainsharing system to encourage responsibility and recognition. They would make sure that everyone had a chance for meaningful achievement at work. They would be careful not to use gainsharing to create greater insecurity (by putting pay at risk). They would not view money as a motivator.

What Can Managers Do to Motivate?

As researchers have explored human motivation at work, they have also studied and written about the nature of management, trying to discover what a manager should or should not do to increase the motivation of the work force. Managers' assumptions about the nature of people at work have a tremendous effect on how they attempt to motivate others. For example, one organization that was exploring gainsharing decided not to pursue the idea further when the president of the organization said, "I do not believe in gainsharing. I grew up in the Depression. Having a job is the only gain anyone needs." He assumed that his work force shared his views. He believed that their need for security would produce motivation. He clung to his assumptions, even though most of his work force was younger and had never experienced the Great Depression. He clung to his assumptions even though they were not supported by Herzberg's research.

Managers' assumptions are also influenced by the predominant management gurus of their time. As this chapter is being written, management thought is dominated by the work of W. Edwards Deming, Tom Peters, and Stephen Covey. These writers stress the importance of employee involvement and participatory management. However, many of today's practicing managers were influenced by other writers and other philosophies that do not place a value on employee involvement and participation. Their philosophies are in conflict with current management thought. Frequently, they rely on punishment and rewards as the primary motivators at work.

There are those who still follow the theories of Frederick Taylor, one of the earliest and most influential writers about the role of management. Some even credit Taylor with coining the term "gainsharing." His book, *The Principles of Scientific Management*, written in the early 1900s, influenced a generation of managers and launched industrial engineering as a profession. The book explains how to use the principles of scientific management to motivate a steelworker to work harder by offering him more money for loading pig iron. He illustrates with an actual quote from a conversation he had with the steelworker.

> You will do exactly as this man (manager) tells you tomorrow, from morning till night. When he tells you to pick up a pig and walk, you pick it up and you walk, and when he tells you to sit down and rest, you sit down. You do that straight through the day. And what's more no backtalk. Now a high-priced man does just what he is told to do and no backtalk. Do you understand that? When the man tells you to walk, you walk, when he tells you to sit down, you sit down, and you don't talk back to him.[7]

Scientific management assumes that some people in an organization are better at thinking while others should simply do what they are told (without talking back). Money and punishment are seen as the most powerful motivators. Workers are viewed as lazy and unwilling to do their best without management intervention. It is assumed that the average worker does not seek more responsibility and in fact will avoid responsibility. Douglas McGregor, the great scholar of organizations many years later, would call these assumptions "Theory X."

Management assumptions are critical to gainsharing success. Assumptions are like lenses in a pair of glasses. They will distort, focus, and alter everything a manager sees. For example, a small Michigan manufacturing company was purchased by a group of investors who had experience with the Scanlon gainsharing system. The investors specialized in turnaround situations. The investors' assumptions about management were not "Theory X." The gainsharing approach they selected was highly participatory and involved the union and the employees in solving company problems. Within three years the company was highly profitable, having carved out a niche by competing head-to-head with the much larger 3M Corporation. The company became so successful that the investors decided to sell, receiving a tenfold return on their investment. The Theory X purchasers did not believe in the value of participatory management. Their assumptions distorted their view of the gainsharing system. They saw the bonuses as giving away some of their profits and saw the frequent meetings required for participation as a waste of time and a loss of their management power. Within two years, the gainsharing system was in ruins, employee morale was at an all-time low, and the new owners were debating moving the plant south to avoid their union.

Today, "Taylorism" has fallen out of favor, but its basic assumptions continue to drive many management actions. Theory X managers usually do not support gainsharing if there is an employee involvement component, yet they may embrace gainsharing as a compensation approach. They tend to support gainsharing systems where pay is at risk. In these systems employees are not paid a market wage, but are able to reach or surpass market rates with the addition of a gainsharing bonus. These assumptions are the same assumptions that drove Taylor's piecework systems in the early 1900s. The assumptions driving these systems are that people do not want to work, that money is the primary motivator, that employees will not work hard unless their paychecks are at risk, and that management must intervene by designing a more effective carrot if workers are to be motivated to work.

While McGregor studied managers with Theory X assumptions, he also studied managers with the opposite assumptions about people. McGregor called these assumptions "Theory Y." These managers assume that workers want to accept more responsibility, actually enjoy work, want to set their own goals, have great ambition, and can be trusted. Today, most modern management practices such as TQM, teams, employee involvement, etc., are based on Theory Y assumptions. Few managers realize that McGregor developed Theory Y by studying a variety of organizations with Scanlon gainsharing systems. McGregor endorsed Scanlon by saying, "I need only mention the Scanlon (gainsharing) Plan as the outstanding embodiment of these ideas in practice." Herman Miller, a Michigan office furniture manufacturer, has had a Scanlon gainsharing system since the 1950s. Consistently ranked as one of America's most admired corporations, the company has been a leader in Theory Y management practices. Former CEO Hugh De Pree describes the essence of Theory Y management: "The difference at Herman Miller is not the lengthened shadow of one man nor the talents of an elite group of managers. The difference is the energy beamed from thousands of unique contributions by people who understand, accept, and are committed to the idea they can make a difference."[8]

Is Money the Universal Motivator?

The assumptions behind the Scanlon gainsharing system are congruent with the work of McGregor, Maslow, and Herzberg. Scanlon systems are based on the assumption that people want to participate and accept responsibility. Other gainsharing systems were developed based on different assumptions about human motivation. Mitchell Fein, the creator of the Improshare® gainsharing system, wrote: "Herzberg's postulation that money is not a motivator, that the work itself motivates, was sweet music to managers' ears. Not only did workers not accept these notions; neither did management."[9]

Fein assumes that money is the primary motivator. While Improshare® encourages employee involvement, it is not viewed as the critical component that it is in Scanlon gainsharing systems. Fein cites his own studies, which indicate the Improshare® system motivates and creates greater productivity without the need for employee involvement. The debate has taken on renewed vigor as a result of the work of the late W. Edwards Deming. Deming, the great quality expert, had very strong feelings about motivation and the role of money as a motivator. He believed in the power of intrinsic motivation. He believed that individual merit pay systems, rewards, punishment, and most of the other motivators used in business were dysfunctional. He believed in Theory Y management. Deming summed up over 50 years of organizational study by saying, "Pay is not a motivator."

If pay is not a motivator, why is it so common? Voltaire said, "When it is a question of money, everybody is of the same religion." Leavitt writes: "Money incentives have come to occupy a central place because money is a common means for satisfying all sorts of diverse needs in our society and because money may be handled and measured. Money is 'real'; it is communicable. Many other means to need-satisfaction are abstract and ephemeral."[10]

Jerry McAdams in *The Reward Plan Advantage* takes a pragmatic approach that seeks the middle ground.[11] He does not take the extreme position of Deming or Kohn that all motivation is intrinsic, nor does he endorse the assumptions of Leavitt and Fein that extrinsic monetary rewards are sufficient motivators alone. He believes that a properly designed reward system will avoid the problems of both extremes. McAdams' credibility is enhanced by the fact that he was the head researcher in several large-scale studies of alternative reward systems for the American Compensation Association.

Because money is universal, quick, and easy, it often becomes the only focus of gainsharing systems. Gainsharing as compensation or a "bonus" is easier to design, communicate, and administer than is a more comprehensive method such as Scanlon. Scanlon practitioners have found that the real value of financial rewards is not the money they provide per se, but rather the way in which the money helps to focus employees and management on business issues. In fact, Scanlon practitioners no longer view Scanlon as simple gainsharing, as a plan, or as a program. They consider Scanlon to be a *process* for organizational and individual development. Each part of the process is important for success. Scanlon practitioners believe that most gainsharing systems have fatal flaws built into them. Typical gainsharing approaches that consider money to be the only motivator can motivate only when there are bonuses to be paid. They do not provide motivation during tough times, when a company cannot pay bonuses but needs motivated employees the most. Many operate like a lottery. Employees enjoy the opportunity to earn extra money but believe the bonus is subject to change. They do not believe they can influence the results. Their focus on gainsharing as a program or a plan, instead of a *process or system*, prevents them from adapting and changing, which creates built-in obsolescence.

There appears to be a basic paradox among gainsharing practitioners. Gainsharing is viewed as a solution for motivating workers by managers with totally opposite assumptions about what motivates workers. Each camp has its own management theorists to justify its assumptions. Each is able to cite objective studies to validate its position. Gainsharing systems are not created equal. Those exploring gainsharing must first determine their own basic assumptions about human motivation and then design a gainsharing process based on those assumptions. If they work with an existing gainsharing process or gainsharing consultant, they must question whether the process or the consultant share their assumptions.

When management assumptions and gainsharing systems match, there is power, synergy, and integrity. Gainsharing becomes a way for the manager to manage. When management assumptions and gainsharing do not match, gainsharing is not effective. Gainsharing sends a strong message to the organization about what behaviors are important. Employees are quick to find inconsistencies between what the managers say and what gainsharing rewards. While this is not to say that consistency per se makes gainsharing successful, inconsistencies will soon undermine even the best gainsharing process.

Explore Your Options

The following questions and suggestions are designed to help you explore your assumptions and determine what gainsharing approach is congruent with your assumptions. Because Scanlon and Improshare® are the only classic approaches still being installed, they are highlighted. If the reader is evaluating another approach or designing a generic gainsharing process, use the questions to help clarify your thinking.

A (Assumptions)

When evaluating your options, consider the following questions:

Do you believe workers are motivated more by extrinsic rewards or intrinsic rewards?

- If extrinsic, design a gainsharing process that focuses on money as a motivator. Consider Improshare®.

- If intrinsic, maybe you should not even consider gainsharing. If you do, consider a process that takes into consideration intrinsic motivators like participation. Consider Scanlon.

Do you agree with Herzberg that the human motivators are responsibility, achievement, recognition, and satisfaction with the work itself?

- If yes, build your plan to include these motivators. Consider Scanlon.

- If no, what do you believe are the needs of your work force? If you believe money is a universal need, design a process with a large bonus component. Consider Improshare®.

Do you believe in Theory X or Theory Y management?

- If X, consider scientific management. Consider designing a piecework system instead of gainsharing. Consider automation or contracting out as a way to increase productivity and quality. Consider putting a large part of your employees' wages at risk. Consider a merit system instead of a gainsharing system.

- If Y, involve your employees in designing the process. Do not use money as the only source of motivation. Use gainsharing to build participation and commitment. Include all employees in the gainsharing pool. Consider Scanlon.

B (Business Literacy)

One of the hottest management ideas of the late 1990s is the idea of business literacy, or "open-book management." Authors such as John Case, Jack Stack, and John Schuster have done a wonderful job of documenting the effects literacy training has had on a wide variety of organizations. Stack's own organization, Springfield ReManufacturing Corporation, has become one of the most sought-after places for a benchmark visit because of its amazing turnaround story.

What these open-book managers and authors have discovered is the power generated when employees know their business, are provided meaningful information on the performance of their business, are able to influence decisions to improve their business, and are included in the rewards of capitalism. Open-book practitioners seek to create companies where every employee is a business person.

Despite the hype, these ideas are not new. Many were developed over half a century ago by Joseph Scanlon, the father of gainsharing, and are incorporated in every Scanlon gainsharing process. Scanlon was an eclectic man. During his lifetime he was a steelworker, union leader, cost accountant, prizefighter, researcher, and lecturer at the Massachusetts Institute of Technology (MIT). His name has become synonymous with gainsharing.

During the Depression, Scanlon learned the value of cooperation by helping unemployed steelworkers find land and seed for gardens. After the Depression, he found himself on the union bargaining committee in negotiations with his employer, Empire Sheet and Tube. Barely profitable, Empire was not able to increase wages and was in danger of going under. In desperation, Scanlon sought advice from the International Brotherhood of Steelworkers. He was told to return to Empire to see if there was any way the workers could improve the company in hope of making it more profitable. The workers had many ideas for improving the company, and Empire was saved. News of Scanlon's work spread, and soon he was helping other workers and their companies cooperate to survive.

The initial Scanlon Plans had no "gainsharing" bonus formula. They focused on business literacy and employee involvement. As companies became stronger and survival was no longer the issue, the idea of sharing gains was born. The initial gainsharing formulas were designed to share improvements in labor productivity. As workers were able to reduce the cost of labor, these savings were split, with 25% of the savings going to the company and 75% going to the workers. The plans were very successful. Scanlon was asked to join the Steelworkers Research Department.

With the outbreak of World War II, Scanlon became involved in creating joint union and management councils to help with the war effort. After the war, labor and management were no longer interested in cooperation. Scanlon was asked by Douglas McGregor to join the faculty of MIT, where he was involved in establishing gainsharing systems until his death in 1956. Russell Davenport reported on the philosophy, methods, and potential of Scanlon's ideas in "The Greatest Opportunity on Earth" and "Enterprise for Everyman," two *Fortune* magazine articles in 1949 and 1950.[12] Scanlon's work was continued by Carl Frost and Fred Lesieur. Frost contributed to Scanlon theory and practice by creating the Frost/Scanlon principles. Lesieur worked with MIT and specialized in installing Scanlon Plans in companies with unions.

The Scanlon process has survived for over half a century, and many of America's "best" organizations use Scanlon. Motorola, Herman Miller, Dana, Donnelly, Sears, Magna Copper, Beth Israel Hospital, and Whirlpool are just a few of the organizations that were influenced by Scanlon's ideas. Scanlon never trademarked his process or copyrighted his ideas, believing they should be made freely available. Today, many generic plans (and some trademarked plans) are really Scanlon Plans. Scanlon Plans are a combination of philosophy (Theory Y), principles, and common-sense practices.

Reflecting his basic belief in business literacy and employee involvement, Scanlon wrote:

> What we are trying to say is simply this: That the average worker knows his own job better than anyone else, and that there are a great many things that he could do if he has a complete understanding of the necessary. Given this opportunity of expressing his intelligence and ingenuity, he becomes a more useful and more valuable citizen in any given community or in any industrial operation.[13]

The primary Scanlon principle is called Identity. The principle of Identity incorporates what writers are today calling business literacy. Through a process of education, all employees are taught about their company, their competitors, and the need to change. Each Scanlon company develops its own process to insure Identity. Visits by customers, information on competitors, and training on how to read financial reports are all ways that Scanlon companies create Identity. Beth Israel Hospital implements Identity by sharing hospital information with its employees in three languages (French, Spanish, and English). Sears creates Identity by having employees complete "learning maps," customized colorful interactive visuals that teach employees "What Day It Is on Retail Street," "The Voices of Our Customers," and "The Sears Money Flow." Each company designs an Identity process that fits its industry and size.

When evaluating your options, consider the following questions:

Do you believe that business literacy among all employees in your company or organization is important?

- If yes, consider developing a gainsharing process that stresses the importance of business literacy. This can be done through training, but also through systems that encourage business literacy, e.g., screening committees or Great Game of Business® financial reporting systems. Include developing business literacy as part of the installation strategy of your gainsharing process. Consider Scanlon.

- If no, focus your system on the financial reward potential of gainsharing. Consider Improshare®.

Are you willing to share financial and operational data with your employees?

- If yes, read the open-book management literature for ideas on how to do this. Consider Scanlon.
- If no, business literacy is not for you! Scanlon is not for you.

C (Commitment)

Organizations are changing their commitments to customers, investors, and employees. The quality movement has helped world-class organizations increase their commitment to customers. Investors, led by large institutions, have demanded and received increased commitment to their needs. Paradoxically, during these times of increased commitment to customers and investors, organizations are decreasing their commitment to employees. Many employees work part-time, their organizations unable or unwilling to commit to full-time employment. Full-time employees are told it is impossible for their organizations to commit to lifetime employment. Organizations that have become flatter and leaner cannot even commit to regular advancement for good performers.

While employees are told to expect less organizational commitment, they are asked to commit to new forms of work. They are asked to commit to longer hours and more responsibility. They are expected to commit to being flexible. They are told to commit to lifetime learning to master ever-more complex and changing jobs.

Albert Camus said, "Commitment is the soul of work." Johann Goethe said, "Until one is committed, there is hesitancy, the chance to draw back, always ineffectiveness, concerning all acts of initiative (and creation). There is one elementary truth the ignorance of which kills countless ideas and splendid plans: That the moment one definitely commits oneself, then providence moves too."

The various gainsharing approaches differ in the commitment they make and the commitment they seek. Those that are implemented as a compensation strategy commit to pay a bonus when certain performance targets are met. This in and of itself is a major commitment, just like a commitment to meet payroll or to fund benefits. Once an organization commits to gainsharing, it must follow through with the commitment. A bonus cannot be promised and then withdrawn later. Most gainsharing systems are self-funding, paying for their administration and the bonuses out of gains or savings, yet even these systems demand organizational commitment. For example, Lincoln Electric had to borrow money to meet bonus commitments. Its system paid a bonus based on productivity gains. Employees improved productivity, yet the company was not profitable. This does not happen often, but if it does illustrate the point that a commitment to a bonus is a commitment that must be honored in good times and bad.

Gainsharing systems such as Scanlon that are fundamentally organizational and individual development systems demand great commitment from employees and their organizations. They demand personal and organizational commitment to participation, to fairness, and to increased competency.

Gainsharing and Commitment

Commitment to Participation

Every gainsharing system seeks to alter the commitment of individuals. As a result of gainsharing, individuals are assumed to participate in some way to making the group or organization better. The various approaches differ on how widely to encourage participation and on who is included in the gainsharing group. Some focus only on the production people in an organization and do not include administrative staff or managers. Some focus on teams, with each team operating its own bonus system. Some focus on multiple plants or sites. Gainsharing writers call this the "line of sight" issue. People want to be able to influence the results of a bonus. The more people that are involved, the more difficult this becomes. The less a bonus measure is influenced by participation, the harder it is to explain and to enlist support. For example, employees in a manufacturing operation might feel that they can participate in reducing scrap; yet they may feel they have no control over profits, even though the two measures are related.

The question of who to include in the gainsharing group becomes a question of philosophy and pragmatism. The Scanlon philosophy is to include as many as possible. Thus all levels and jobs are usually identified as participants. This creates a "we are all in it together" state of mind. It makes it easier for departments and teams to work together because they share the same Scanlon bonus. It allows white- and blue-collar workers to find common ground. In large organizations such as Sears (with over 300,000 employees), the group has been defined as a specific store or store support service unit. This fits Sears' organizational structure and allows for a manageable size. In smaller organizations, the group may be defined as the entire organization. Sometimes even part-time employees and key vendors are included in the process.

Commitment to participation can be built into gainsharing or it can be left to chance. For example, historically the Scanlon approach encourages participation through a suggestion system and committee structure. Employees submit suggestions to a production committee made up of coworkers and managers who decide whether to implement the suggestions. Production committees are workgroup- or department-based. Production committees send representatives to a screening committee made up of top management and union leaders. The screening committee reviews suggestions that were rejected and those suggestions that involve multiple departments or large expenditures of money to implement. This system exists in many organizations as well as some newer forms of participation such as work teams and Kaizan teams.

Employees in Scanlon companies are expected to participate by "influencing decisions in their areas of competence." The commitment to participation is evident in the way the Scanlon process is implemented. Scanlon Plans are not purchased off-the-shelf from consultants or third parties. They are not implemented unless there is evidence of virtually universal organizational commitment at all levels. The process begins with discussions at the top level of the organization. Every top leader, after learning about the Scanlon process, is asked to make a personal and professional commitment of support. Only when the top-level team is personally and professionally committed is the Scanlon process introduced to the other levels of the organization. If there is a union, the union leadership is introduced to the idea. Eventually all levels of management, including the front-line supervisors, are introduced to the concepts of Scanlon and asked to make a personal and professional commitment of support. When the managers representing the organization, their departments, and their professions have committed and the union leadership has committed, the process is explained to the rank-and-file employees. They too are asked to commit to creating a different way of working through the Scanlon process. They vote to participate by electing a committee to design the Scanlon system. After it is designed, the committee presents its work to all of the employees, and a vote to try Scanlon for a trial period is taken. Acceptance levels of 80-90% are usually required for the process to be implemented. Finally, after the trial period, the Scanlon process is evaluated one more time and a vote is taken to continue Scanlon indefinitely as a way of working together.

This process is time-consuming. It takes an average of 35 weeks from initial exploration until Scanlon is approved for the trial period. The process is designed not for speed but rather for building commitment and participation. The result is:

- The process builds commitment: People "own" the Scanlon process, even giving it a unique name such as UNITE, PRIDE, REACH, or I.C.E.

- The process does not belong to one department, e.g., Human Resources.

- The process prevents Scanlon from becoming another "flavor of the month" approach.

- The process requires an organization to spend time up front explaining gainsharing rather than risking that people will understand later once it is in place.

- The process prevents one-size-fits-all mistakes because each company is treated as the unique entity it is.

- The process builds internal competence. A company does not become dependent on consultants or others to maintain or improve the system. Employees grow as human beings as they learn new skills.

- The process creates the links and support needed for implementation as well as design.

- The process creates a model that can be used when it needs to be renewed.

- The process leads to success: a study done at the University of Wisconsin found that participation, voting, and plan understanding were highly correlated with gainsharing success.[14]

The idea of employee voting is intimidating to some, especially with an 80–90% approval rate recommended. However, the vote rarely fails. More typically, as the Scanlon process unfolds, issues will surface that may require a delay or change in the process. For example, one company decided not to pursue Scanlon because it was involved in ISO certification and the top managers did not feel they could handle both initiatives at the same time. Once ISO was completed, the company began the Scanlon process. Others may decide not to continue because the union will not support gainsharing or the top management team cannot accept Theory Y management practices. The commitment level the process generates is illustrated by what happened in a recent Sears installation. A long-term employee became sick and was taken to the hospital on the day the vote was to be taken. She called from her hospital bed because she wanted the vote to be unanimous.

Other gainsharing approaches require little commitment to participate from employees. They are designed by internal or external consultants and then simply communicated to employees. They can be installed quickly. There is no vote. They can be changed quickly and easily. They do not create commitment.

The issues surrounding participation and gainsharing are similar to the issues surrounding participation and employee stock ownership. Participation is not required for gainsharing nor is it required for ownership. Participation is linked to the strategy or reason for adopting gainsharing as it is linked to the reasons for adopting ESOPs. Some gainsharing systems are viewed as a compensation strategy, and participation is not required. Some ESOPs are viewed as a tax-saving strategy, and participation is not required. Research on both gainsharing and employee stock ownership have found that effectiveness is increased when combined with participation.

When evaluating your options, consider the following questions:

Do you wish to commit to participation?

- If yes, consider designing participation into the system from the beginning by having employees create the system. Make sure top leadership is committed to making gainsharing a success. Consider Scanlon.

- If no, Improshare® may still require more participation than you feel comfortable with. Do *not* consider Scanlon.

Do you have time for participation?

- If yes, consider a process like Scanlon.

- If no, wait until you have time. You simply cannot have meaningful participation if you do not take the time.

Commitment to Equity (Fairness)

Scanlon gainsharing systems define equity (in the sense of fairness and impartiality, not an ownership interest) as a genuine commitment to accounting for the needs of all constituents, including customers, investors, and employees. The pursuit of equity is the way the Scanlon gainsharing system holds everyone accountable to the stakeholders. Scanlon is the only gainsharing process that defines these multiple accountabilities, yet the idea is probably as old as time itself. Confucius was reported to have said, "The proper man understands equity, the small man profits." Equity is important because a focus on only one or two of the stakeholders will ultimately destroy an organization. For example, the auto industry in the U.S. historically has been a good place to work, with high pay and good benefits. It has also been a good place to invest, yet consumers began switching en masse to Japanese automobiles in the 1970s because they were not happy with the quality and service of U.S. companies. The U.S. was close to losing the industry until the auto companies and their employees made the gut-wrenching changes needed to compete. There are companies whose profitability is unacceptably low or nonexistent, yet whose employees demand higher and higher wages, eventually forcing the company to go out of business. Today, there are companies that lay off their employees even though they are highly profitable, with record sales. Such companies are liquidating their human assets and setting in motion their own demise.

Carl Frost, in describing the Scanlon equity process, wrote:

> During the early days of Scanlon and somewhat persistently since, many have defined equity as bonuses. The early days were adversarial. Wages were not nationally uniform or substantial. Too often management permitted and even encouraged the expectation of supplemental income, primarily as a result of productivity improvements, i.e., Improshare®, gainsharing. The use of the word share often suggests difference and division rather than neutrality of benefits that are mutually inclusive rather than exclusive.[15]

Scanlon companies operationalize the equity concept by creating appropriate reliable databases of customer satisfaction, financial performance, and human resources. There are regular, public occasions where the data are shared and discrepancies between what is and what needs to be are explored. Sometimes positive discrepancies are noted, and sometimes negative discrepancies are found. Frequently, bonus formulas are constructed that take into account the needs of all stakeholders. Sears has developed a "Total Performance Index" as a component of corporate transformation. The vision is to make Sears a compelling place to shop, to work, and to invest. Customer, employee, and investor measures are tracked. Spring Engineering and Manufacturing Company even named their Scanlon system the I.C.E. (Investor, Customer, and Employee) Plan to emphasize equity. The Scanlon Equity Principle includes many concepts business writers are now calling a "balanced scorecard."

Bonus formulas that take into account the needs of all stakeholders are better than those that emphasize only one. The Lincoln Electric bonus, mentioned earlier, might satisfy employees but may not meet the needs of investors. One company paid a bonus to employees for improvement in quality, yet the firm's customers said the company's quality standards were too low. The company found itself rewarding employees for performance that its customers would not accept. These examples illustrate the difficulty in creating equity. It is much easier to simply create a bonus. However, an equity system is superior to a bonus system alone because equity provides the greatest long-term organizational security. Those involved in Scanlon gainsharing find that the primary reason employees are interested in developing a Scanlon process is to provide long-term employment security and not to provide short-term bonuses.

Companies that stress a bonus create employees who are dissatisfied when the bonus cannot be paid. These employees are conditioned to expect a bonus. They are not aware that their investors may be losing money or that their customers have gone somewhere else. In companies committed to equity, employees know the needs of the other stakeholders and are willing to make sacrifices when necessary.

Organizations operationalize the principle of equity in many ways. Traditionally, they decide what to measure and then construct a historical baseline that represents the current level of the measure(s). When the measure(s) is exceeded, the gain is split between the company and the employees. Operational measures such as labor productivity, scrap, safety, or quality measures are typical. Financial measures such as profit, ROI (return on investment), or EVA (economic value added) are also used. American Compensation Association survey results indicate that organizations report greater success with measures that take into account both operational and financial measures.[16] The employees' portion of the gain is placed in a bonus pool and is distributed either on a percentage basis of salary or on "hours worked." (The Fair Labor Standards Act regulates how nonexempt employee bonuses are computed and should be consulted before designing a bonus formula.) Almost always the bonus is paid monthly or quarterly. Often, a portion of the employees' share is put in a reserve account and used to cover any future deficits. At the end of the year, any remaining reserves are then returned to the employees. The most typical way the bonus is paid is through a separate check. These methods have withstood the test of time because they are considered fair and reasonable and are usually not difficult to design and compute.

Increasingly, some organizations take a quite different approach. They look *forward* and ask the question, "What performance is needed to achieve our objectives in the upcoming period?" They believe what was adequate in the past may no longer be adequate for the future. They do not wish to reward for improvements if the results still do not meet the continuous improvement goals they have committed to. This system is called "goal sharing" and is the approach favored by Sears and Spring Engineering. Both organizations participatively set the goals with their employees so that the employees know the goals are achievable and realistic.

Both the gainsharing and goalsharing approaches can be used by not-for-profit organizations, although unfortunately there are few examples. One of the most well known is Beth Israel Hospital–Boston, which has had a successful Scanlon system called "Prepare 21" since 1989. Beth Israel has credited its Scanlon process with helping save hundreds of thousands of dollars in cost while improving quality and patient care. One of the highlights of Beth Israel's year is the Prepare 21 Recognition program. During this time, employees and teams are recognized for their contribution to Prepare 21 and to Beth Israel. It is usually standing-room only as the busy staff of this major teaching hospital comes together to honor its own. Recipients not only receive the accolades of their peers but also have their names added permanently to a special kiosk near the hospital's cafeteria.

Other organizations feel that the only true measure of performance is profit, and so they develop profit sharing plans. Purists would argue that profit sharing is a concept foreign to a discussion of gainsharing, but philosophically the ideas are similar. Profit sharing can be considered a financial measure bonus system. Profits above a base number are split with employees. Scanlon studied profit sharing in the 1940s and concluded: "The analysis of these plans indicates that a sense of participation and partnership is the fundamental prerequisite. If this is fully developed the type of plan itself is of secondary importance."[17]

Douglas Kruse found that the adoption of profit sharing results in productivity gains of 3.5% to 5%.[18] There are two common challenges associated with profit sharing. The first is a literacy issue. Most employees simply do not understand profit and must be educated to understand what it is. The second issue is "line of sight." Profit is influenced by many factors beyond the control of the typical employee.

These challenges are not impossible, and there are many successful profit sharing programs. Wescast Industries, a Canadian company that produces most of the engine manifolds in North America, combines a once-a-year profit sharing bonus with a quarterly operational measure bonus system. This system helps to focus employees on the profitability of the corporation and at the same time on the need for quality, safety, and productivity.

Employee ownership can be combined with gainsharing, goalsharing, and profit sharing. Herman Miller has had a Scanlon system since 1950, and also provides stock to every employee with over one year of service. Max De Pree, a former CEO of Herman Miller, said, "Employee stock ownership is clearly a competitive reality. Nothing is being given. Ownership is earned and paid for. The heart of it is profit sharing, and there is no sharing if there are no profits. Risk and reward are connected logically and fairly. There is no smug condescension at play here. Rather, there is a certain morality in connecting shared accountability as employees with shared ownership. This lends a rightness and permanence to the relationship of each of us to our work and to each other."[19]

Finally, it is not necessary and maybe even counterproductive to give money as the gain. Once a bonus check is cashed and the money spent, it is often difficult for employees to know where the money went. Cerdec Corporation/Drakenfeld Products provides its employees with "mall dollars" that they can spend at local businesses. Employees can purchase goods and services from vacations to cars. A new VCR may have more "trophy value" than the equivalent in money. Employees remember what items they received in mall dollars. Enterprising organizations could even use the mall dollar concept to negotiate favorable exchanges and discounts from merchants. Most merchants would gladly offer a discount for a captive customer. An additional benefit of the concept is that money remains in the local economy.

Another creative approach is taken by Weyburn-Bartel Incorporated, which pays its bonus in meat. Employees sign up for various cuts of beef or seafood that are delivered by refrigerated truck. The system prevents the value of their bonus from being eroded by sales taxes. While this approach is not for everyone, it does show that there are many creative ways to create an equity system.

When evaluating your options, consider the following questions:

Do you wish to create a bonus system or an equity system?

- If bonus, consider Improshare®.

- If equity, consider Scanlon. Create a balanced scorecard measuring system. Make sure the bonus formula takes into account the real needs of the stakeholders. Think creatively.

Do you wish to implement gainsharing, goalsharing, or profit sharing?

- If gainsharing, you will need good historical data from which to create a baseline. Select a baseline period that takes into account your business cycle and typical performance.

- If goalsharing, you will need to participatively develop goals with employees if you want them to be realistic and accepted.

- If profit sharing, you will need to determine what measure of profit you will use. You will have to determine what level of profit will result in sharing.

Commitment to Competency

Business literacy, participation, and Theory Y management require increased employee competency. Employees must learn to do more than what is expected in traditional firms. Motorola's Scanlon philosophy has led it to invest over 50 million dollars per year (as of 1990) in employee training and development. Sears has created Sears University. When implemented as a compensation strategy, gainsharing does not identify this type of commitment to increased competency as one of its goals.

Participatory gainsharing requires changes in both managers and employees. Managers must learn how to lead, to listen, and to coach. Employees must learn how to work in teams, control quality, and reduce costs. Both employees and organizations must commit to major investments in time, energy, and money to be successful. Scanlon organizations believe the investment is worth the cost. They believe employees are an asset to be developed, not a cost to be reduced. For example, in three separate audits Motorola calculated a $30 return for every dollar invested in training and development.

At the very least, every gainsharing system must help employees to become competent in understanding the basis of the gainsharing formula that is used. If employees do not understand the calculation, they will not know why they are or are not receiving the bonus. They will view the bonus as a lottery that they hope to win but over which they have little influence.

When evaluating your options, consider the following questions:

Do you believe employees are an asset to be developed or a cost to be reduced?

- If an asset to be developed, recognize your strategy is for the long term. Consider a Scanlon process.

- If a cost to be reduced, do not consider gainsharing. Consider reengineering, automation, contracting out, or another approach as a strategy.

Mechanics of Gainsharing

Once an organization is clear on the ABCs of gainsharing, the mechanics of gainsharing become more straightforward. Every organization considering a gainsharing system should address the following mechanics before implementing it.

I. What is our reason for considering a gainsharing system; i.e., what do we seek to accomplish?

II. Do we have top management and organization commitment and support?

III. Is this the right time?
- A. Do we have enough time to design the system?
- B. Are there other issues we need to address first?
  1. Management competency
  2. Union relations
  3. Compensation system

IV. Who will create the system?
- A. Will we work with a consultant?
- B. Will we design it ourselves?
  1. How will we select the design committee(s) and what will their roles be?
  2. How will we involve the organization/union?

V. What are we trying to improve?
- A. How will we measure it?
- B. Will we have all stakeholders identified?

VI. Improvement over what?
- A. Gainsharing
  1. How will we construct the base period?
  2. What is the protection for the company?
     a. Split
     b. Reserve
     c. Caps
- B. Goalsharing
  1. How much money can we spend?
  2. What are the goals we must accomplish?
  3. How will we pay out?
- C. Profit sharing
  1. What measure of profitability will we use?
  2. How will we protect the company?
     a. Minimum profitability before sharing
     b. Split
     c. Reserves
     d. Caps

VII. Who will be covered by gainsharing?
    A.   Will we include everybody?
    B.   How will we take into consideration line-of-sight?
VIII. How will we communicate gainsharing to our employees?
  IX. Who will maintain the system?
    A.   Do we need a gainsharing coordinator position?
    B.   How will we keep it from becoming another Human Relations department program?
   X. How will we know if gainsharing is successful?
  XI. How will we change the system?

Conclusion

Gainsharing is a proven, powerful tool to manage an organization if there is an understanding of the basic ABCs of gainsharing. Mistakes are made by those that do not take the time to understand the differences between the various approaches that are available. Before beginning a gainsharing program, carefully evaluate your Assumptions about motivation. Consider the effect of Business literacy. Finally, consider the level of Commitment your organization will expect and is willing to provide. Once the basic ABCs are mastered, the right gainsharing approach for you will be much clearer.

Notes

1. Robert Levering and Milton Moskowitz, *The 100 Best Companies to Work For in America* (New York: Doubleday, 1993).

2. Jerry L. McAdams and Elizabeth J. Hawk, *Organizational Performance and Rewards: 663 Experiences in Making the Link* (St. Louis, Mo.: American Compensation Association and Maritz, Inc., 1994).

3. M. Schuster, "Forty Years of Scanlon Plan Research: A Review of the Descriptive and Empirical Literature," *International Yearbook of Organizational Democracy* 1 (1983): 53-71.

4. Dong-One Kim, "Factors Influencing Organizational Performance in Gainsharing Programs" (unpublished paper, University of Wisconsin-Madison, 1994).

5. Alfie Kohn, *Punished by Rewards: The Trouble with Gold Stars, Incentive Plans, A's, Praise, and Other Bribes* (New York: Houghton Mifflin Company, 1993), 190.

6. Lewis Eigen and Jonathan P. Siegel, *The Manager's Book of Quotations* (New York: AMACOM, 1989), 271.

7. Frederick Winslow Taylor, *The Principles of Scientific Management* (1911).

8. Hugh De Pree, *Business as Unusual: The People and Principles of Herman Miller* (Zeeland: Herman Miller, 1986), 4.

9. Mitchell Fein, *Improshare: An Alternative to Traditional Managing* (American Institute of Industrial Engineers, 1981), 27.

10. Ibid., 23.

11. Jerry L. McAdams, *The Reward Plan Advantage* (San Francisco: Jossey-Bass, 1996).

12. R. Davenport, "The Greatest Opportunity on Earth," *Fortune*, October 1949; idem, "Enterprise for Everyman," *Fortune*, vol. 41, no. 1 (January 1950), 51-58.

13. Joseph Scanlon, personal correspondence, Penn State University, Steelworkers Archives.

14. Kim, "Factors Influencing Organizational Performance in Gainsharing Programs."

15. Carl Frost, "Leadership in the New American Workplace," unpublished workbook. (Scanlon Plan Associates, 1993).

16. McAdams and Hawk, *Organizational Performance and Rewards.*

17. Joseph Scanlon, "Profit Sharing under Collective Bargaining: Three Case Studies," in *The Scanlon Plan: A Frontier in Labor-Management Cooperation,* ed. Frederick G. Lesieur (Cambridge, MA: Technology Press of MIT, 1958).

18. Douglas Kruse, *Profit Sharing: Does It Make a Difference?* (Kalamazoo, Mich.: W.E. Upjohn Institute for Employment Research, 1993), vi.

19. Max De Pree, *Leadership Is an Art* (New York: Doubleday, 1987), 85. (Max De Pree is not to be confused with his brother Hugh [cited above], who preceded him as Herman Miller CEO.)

Part Two

Case Studies

Incentive Compensation and Employee Ownership at SAIC

William H. Scott, Jr.

In an employee ownership company, the question of who owns how much stock is important; however, this chapter argues that healthy stock flows that motivate growth over the long term are much more important. New employees at my employer, Science Applications International Corporation (SAIC), have said, "Employee ownership is about who owns the company. If it isn't me, why should I care?" I claim that leadership, participation, and incentive stock flows can be used to foster an ownership culture that can enable long-term growth. This growth can gradually dilute equity shareholdings from the longer-term owners to new contributors, yet still allow a robust return for the original shareholders.

My background provides a unique perspective on employee ownership. I joined SAIC when it had 20 employees in 1970, and I have worked within its employee ownership culture as SAIC has grown to 22,000 employees in 26 years. We have grown 15% per year for the last 13 years, which means that our revenues have doubled every five years, and our stock price has done nearly as well. As a physicist, I study radiation shielding, and I use the same mathematics and simulation skills employed in the physics of radiation shielding to study equity ownership and growth. I am also SAIC's Participation Advocate, in which capacity I work with many employees and committees to improve our company and our work environment. The purpose of this chapter is to share some of this experience and to encourage your attention to the equity flows that occur from various compensation, bonus, and retirement plans. Leadership, participation, and incentive stock flows are the keys to healthy employee ownership.

Employee ownership exists as a spectrum of partial to total ownership, and there is no agreed-upon definition of what constitutes full employee ownership. My opinion is that in a true employee-owned company, (1) employees own nearly all of the stock, (2) almost all employees own some stock, (3) no one owns very much of the stock, and (4) almost all of this employee ownership is free and clear of leveraged corporate debt. The fourth condition reserves the term "full employee ownership" to those companies who have successfully paid off their leveraged ESOP debt. Under this definition, SAIC may be the world's largest fully employee-owned company.

I think that SAIC employees are quite representative of the new information age worker, so the following ideas should be transferable to many other companies. However, I will refrain from commenting on traditional manufacturing and labor service employees because I have no experience in these fields.

Employee Ownership Culture

SAIC's ownership philosophy is that "those who contribute to the company should own it, and that ownership should be proportional to that contribution and performance as much as feasible."[1] This implies a certain fairness in how we distribute our equity. It also implies the use of equity to motivate employees to work competitively for further growth and profits. This tension between fairness and competitiveness is not generally understood by those outside the employee ownership community. Ownership means little patience with inefficiency or inappropriate efforts. Ownership means staking your future on shareholder value. This puts tremendous pressure on everyone to perform. Equity incentives are not a panacea that makes for easy success. Rather, they can provide extra motivation for employees to work through problems.

There have been several recent unsuccessful attempts at employee ownership. After studying the airline industry, Fred Whittlesey writes: "Possessing common stock does not create ownership, and ownership behaviors may occur without significant stock ownership. Real ownership means real participation in and influence on the business. . . . just as a marriage license does not ensure lifetime marital bliss, realizing the benefits of employee ownership demands more than simply issuing stock to employees."[2] Whittlesey goes on to conclude that much of a true ownership culture is built by the leadership of management over and above actual employee stock ownership.

But what are the desirable features of this true ownership culture? Joseph Blasi is a long-time employee ownership advocate and is perhaps its most constructive critic. Blasi writes: "Over the long run, employee ownership simply will not make sense unless there is a strong culture where employees accept the fact that current income will be deferred and then concentrated in one stock at some risk, but also at some significant reward if the company does well."[3]

Employees would like to think that employee ownership is icing on a cake already made of market-driven wages and benefits. Blasi is skeptical that this would be a recipe for continued success. SAIC employees have shown extraordinary capacity for extra work at specific times to solve specific problems. And if we were to experience a sustained corporate-wide financial downturn, we expect that most of our employees would forego some immediate employment rewards in order to improve the chance of recovery. This willingness for extra work and sacrifice when needed is the essence of Blasi's ownership culture. On the other hand, it is my experience that many of today's employees are much more interested in maximizing their current salary and position within the company than they are in deferring for future payoffs. It may be that those who are more interested in eating their cake now just do not fit well into the employee ownership culture. This chapter will examine the possible stock flows in an employee-owned company and search for those programs that do the most to create an ownership culture.

SAIC's Stock Flow Programs

SAIC's stock programs have evolved over 26 years into a complex set of equity programs. We are not recommending that others try to copy us immediately. However, it is important to understand the diversity, purposes, and stock flows of our various programs to see which might make the most sense for other corporations.

I once examined the stock holdings of terminating SAIC employees to find out how much ownership would retain an employee. There seemed to be no amount of stock for which some employees wouldn't leave if they saw a better opportunity. However, we did find that employees who had been in the company more than three years and had purchased some stock with their own money were 2.5 times less likely to leave than similar employees whose only stock had been given to them. I conclude that the act of paying to obtain ownership goes a lot further than being handed ownership.

Profit Sharing Retirement Plan

SAIC has no defined benefit retirement plan; rather the company annually contributes a reasonable percentage of each eligible employee's salary into a self-directed diversified retirement fund. Each employee makes his or her own investment choices from a family of mutual funds, and SAIC stock is not a choice. The fund vests over several years, assuring long-term employees a modest retirement entirely independent from SAIC performance.

ESOP

A few percent of salary is contributed to our ESOP. Because it has never been leveraged, it functions mostly like a stock bonus plan. Some of our employees just don't want to acquire stock. Jane Bryant Quinn has argued against holding your company's stock, saying, "The purpose of saving is to protect yourself against losing your job. Investing in your company could result in losing your job and your savings at the same time."[4] Our ESOP assures that all eligible employees are owners so that we are not leaving out some employees when we discuss our ownership philosophy. Even though our ESOP contributions are a small part of our stock flows, the fact that all employees are included and the stock stays until retirement or termination means that our ESOP now owns a substantial amount of our total stock.

401(k) Plan

Employees may contribute pretax salary deductions and the company provides a modest match. The employees direct their contributions into diversified mutual funds or into SAIC stock. The company's match is invested entirely in SAIC stock. The 401(k) plan is now the most popular and fastest-growing means of owning company stock. A large fraction of our employees at all salary levels participate. SAIC stock is a popular investment choice, yet nearly half of our 401(k) plan participants are not currently selecting SAIC stock.

Employee Stock Purchase Plan (ESPP)

Employees contribute after-tax dollars from their paychecks to purchase SAIC stock at a small discount. In general, the right to purchase SAIC stock requires a management recommendation. The ESPP and the 401(k) plans allow employees to make limited purchases without management approval. The pretax 401(k) is generally considered to be more efficient than the ESPP, so that many ESPP participants are already contributing the maximum to their 401(k) accounts. However, because 401(k) loan repayments must be counted against an employee's income when qualifying for a mortgage, it may be preferable to save for a residential down payment in the ESPP rather than the 401(k) plan.

Direct Purchases

Each quarter, SAIC's board of directors establishes the fair market price of our stock with a performance formula and the advice of an independent appraiser. A few weeks later, a trade is conducted. All direct shareholders can offer to sell. The retirement plans and employees who have been recommended purchase the stock. Although there is no such requirement, quite often the company balances differences in the trades with repurchases or new issues of stock to stabilize the stock price. Occasionally, sales must be prorated to match buys and sells. We once postponed a trade when there was a large drop in the public stock market between the setting of our stock price and the scheduled trade. Employees sell for their own reasons, such as home purchases, college expenses, or gradual diversification. The plans are the largest purchasers, but new employees and optimistic employees also make substantial purchases when recommended by their management. Generally, all employee purchase requests are approved except for an occasional large request when an employee has received an inheritance or a windfall. Sometimes direct purchases are matched with stock options as a form of an incentive bonus. Our direct purchases and sales bear the closest resemblance to a public stock market, and this liquidity and trust in a fair stock price is very important to a true sense of ownership.

Stock Bonuses

Bonuses are our primary means of motivating key employees and assuring that substantial compensation is based upon performance. Frequently our bonuses are about two-thirds stock with the rest in cash, which pays the taxes and leaves a little for current consumption. Bonuses often include stock options. Bonus and option pools are distributed to groups and divisions within the company based on performance measures, and managers have considerable leeway in establishing their own reward philosophies. Some managers give large bonuses to a few key employees, while others define "key" much more broadly and give many, but smaller, awards. Most bonuses are distributed at year-end when performance is measured; frequently, however, smaller bonuses are awarded for special recognition throughout the year. Stock bonuses can be of unvested stock, which requires four more years of employment before it vests and has full value. We think of the vested stock bonus as recognition of past performance and the unvested bonus as expectation of future performance. The unvested bonus provides more "glue" to retain key employees. The decision to retain rather than sell stock is an ownership choice, so that a bonus of vested stock to newer employees may be more helpful towards building an ownership attitude. Unvested bonuses are better for retaining employees who already have other ownership. Because we allow individual managers to set their own bonus policies, practices vary widely. We also find that when managers are skeptical about the benefits of employee ownership, their employees usually do not end up with as much equity.

Options

Employee stock options are so important that the next section of this chapter will specifically discuss some subtle financial and accounting issues regarding them. At SAIC, we annually award about as many options as are allowed under various state regulations, and we try to award them to the employees most likely to generate revenue and profit growth. About 40% of our employees have received options. Companies that award all their options to only a few top executives must believe that only these executives are responsible for building shareholder value. This thinking is certainly foreign to our experience. It is much easier for top management to build shareholder value when middle management, key employees, and perhaps most other employees are also striving for the same goals. The SAIC option exercise price is always the award date stock price, the term is always five years with four years of vesting, and our options have never finished below the exercise price.

Options are our largest stock flow that transfers equity from today's shareholders to today's performers. Sometimes options are awarded by themselves as naked options, but more often they are combined with purchases or stock bonuses. Options are more effective at motivating employees who do not already hold considerable stock. Recently we have made many of our option grants contingent on meeting specific performance goals such as new revenues or profits.

Employee stock options are a "win-win" bonus. Cash, stock, and option bonuses all transfer value from shareholders to motivate employees, and it is uncertain whether this extra cost will successfully increase shareholder value. Cash and stock bonuses transfer the value immediately. Option value, on the other hand, is contingent on a rising stock price. Therefore, options transfer value from the shareholders only after they have enjoyed a much larger increase in their share value—a win-win transfer. If shareholder value does not increase, the options expire worthless. Thus, options gradually ease the stock price in good times without doing harm in bad times. Unlike cash or stock bonuses, options provide employee motivation without additional risk to the shareholders. Options effectively transfer the bonus risk from the shareholders to the employees. For this reason, many believe that options are much less costly to shareholders than current financial theory indicates.

Incentive Stock Options (ISOs) Versus Nonqualified Options

The two kinds of options have different tax treatments at exercise. The compensation element from nonqualified options is classified as income to the employee and an expense to the company for both personal and corporate tax purposes. The compensation element of an ISO is classified as a capital gain. The conventional wisdom has been that nonqualified options, with their corporate tax deductions, are better for the combination of the company plus the employee than ISOs when the capital gains tax rate is high. However, the purpose of options is to motivate employees, and clearly ISOs are better for the employee. When the capital gains rate was increased, SAIC switched from ISOs to nonqualifieds and increased our number of options.

There are two subtle effects of nonqualifieds that may tip the scales back to ISOs. Because nonqualified value at exercise is considered compensation, the company and employee must pay additional FICA and Medicare taxes. But perhaps more importantly, the stock received from an ISO has a low basis, so that employees are more apt to retain the stock. There are no capital gains consequences of immediately selling the stock from a nonqualified option. Thus, ISOs encourage more retention of company stock.

Deferred Stock Compensation Plan

We have recently adopted a special trust (a rabbi trust) designed to more rapidly build the equity of exceptional new performers with no initial tax consequences. The success of this distribution is yet to be proven, but currently several hundred employees are involved.

Combinations

The bonuses that best build an ownership sense are combinations of the above programs. My personal favorite would be a modest stock bonus, say from 3% to 8% of salary, matched with a cash bonus that pays the income tax on the total bonus, and an option grant comparable to the shares of the stock bonus. The stock bonus should include fully vested stock for newer employees, but could be entirely unvested for those with longer service. Furthermore, I would include an offer to directly purchase a similar number of shares at the next trade, which would be matched with a comparable number of options. This combination bonus, which would include stock, cash, options, and direct purchase, has a strong pay-for-performance aspect; it is designed to build equity, yet it also encourages the further buy-in of a direct purchase.

Anniversary Program

Our stock programs clearly are quite complicated, and we often find that newer employees haven't yet understood the programs. At the first-year anniversary, we offer to let each employee buy about $500 worth of stock and be partially matched with a vesting stock bonus and an option grant. The idea is to make the purchase offer so good that all employees will take the trouble to learn about each of these programs, read the prospectus, and decide to invest. Nevertheless, we are discouraged that only about 25% of eligible employees take this opportunity. Not all employees like the high-performance, high-pressure aspects of employee ownership, and perhaps those who don't invest with this kind of offer just aren't employees who are ready to be motivated by ownership.

Diversification

We have already presented Jane Bryant Quinn's argument not to invest in your company. I disagree with her position. Owners want to invest in themselves and then work hard to assure that their investment is successful. Diversified portfolio theory[5] advises average investors to spread their investments broadly in order to diversify the systematic risk. Some advisors say you should not have more than 5% or 10% of your wealth in any one investment. The same theory would say that if you work in a company and have reason to be optimistic about its prospects, by all means invest strongly. However, when your equity becomes worth several years of salary, portfolio theory would recommend against having more than about 40% of your wealth in company stock, regardless of your optimism. Employee-owned companies should recognize and plan for the needs of the long-term employees to gradually diversify out of large equity holdings. Gifting stock to charities, family members, and trusts is an important way to share wealth with minimum taxes. The direct purchase program should plan for gradual sales from large shareholders. The ESOP should allow diversification, preferably based on equity size although ESOP law only requires diversification based on age. ESOPs of closely held companies can also purchase shares in a section 1042 tax-deferred "rollover" transaction, which allows for tax-advantaged diversification. Incentives other than stock and options will be more effective for large shareholders who are diversifying. The diversification of large shareholders will reduce corporate cash but also will be a significant source of stock to be again awarded to new performers without causing dilution.

Growth Builds Equity and Concentrates the Stock

This section will demonstrate that rational flows of incentive stock coupled with realistic growth scenarios will allow new employees to generate substantial equity holdings if they can continue the growth. A consequence of this successful employee ownership will be a distribution of stock that concentrates the largest holdings with the longest-term employees.

The issue for the new employee is whether the current stock flows are sufficient to build substantial equity over time. Figure 9-1 is a simple exercise in compounding and exponential growth. The assumption is that the stock price grows 12% more than salary growth for 20 years, and that the stock programs continuously provide the employee with 5%, 10%, or 20% of salary worth of stock. Note that after 20 years these stock balances are becoming quite valuable. Five percent is meant to represent an employee who is not aggressively acquiring stock but is obtaining some shares through the ESOP, 401(k), bonuses, payroll deductions, or purchases. The equity worth 4 years of salary after 20 years is building

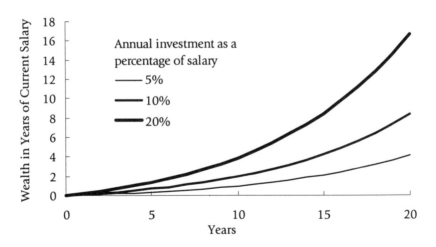

Figure 9-1. Growth in equity as a function of years of 12% continuous growth and investment rates of 5%, 10%, and 20%. The unit of wealth is current wealth divided by current annual salary.

to a reasonable retirement. The 20% curve represents an employee who is both purchasing stock and being awarded reasonable stock bonuses. This has built to substantial wealth (16 years of salary) after 20 years. The middle 10% curve could represent either modest bonuses or active purchases. An important point is that employees acting for themselves through payroll withholding and direct purchases can gain as substantial equity as employees receiving performance bonuses. Also notice that longevity is very important, so that acquiring stock half as rapidly is overcome by 5 years of additional longevity.

The message here for new employees is that with proper stock flows, they can someday have the same equity values as the current long-term employees—if they invest, if they can continue the growth, and if they can stay as long. Figure 9-1 is a simple compounding exercise, but it shows that proper stock flows will allow new employees to anticipate substantial future equity.

At SAIC, we now find that a few percent of employees, mainly those with substantial longevity, own a large fraction of the total stock. Unfortunately, this makes newer employees wonder whether they could ever own as much. In fact, stock concentrations with longevity are actually a natural consequence of a successful employee-owned company.

Let us construct a fictional employee-owned company that compulsively attempts to allocate its stock as evenly as possible. Suppose for simplicity that everyone makes the same salary, that salary stays the same each year, and that there is no employee turnover. Also suppose everyone gets the same annual stock bonus—it is the only way stock is allocated, and the stock bonus is worth the same dollar value each year. Next, as with SAIC, the company's stock value approximately equals its labor base so that the company's bonus rate and an employee's bonus rate are the same, say 4% per year. Finally, the company grows its revenues, profits, employees, and market value at the constant rate of 15% per year by hiring new employees and using them productively. Notice that the stock bonuses will increase the outstanding shares of stock by 4% each year as the total company value grows by 15%. This means that the stock price would increase by 11% each year. This scenario is simple enough to allow an analytic or spreadsheet answer. Yet this compulsively even distribution will still exhibit large stock concentrations because those who have the greatest longevity will own substantially more stock.

Figure 9-2 shows the long-term results for this fictional company, which is not that different from SAIC. Notice the substantial concentration of stock. Just 2.5% of employees own half the stock, 5% of employees own 60%, and the newest 50% of employees own less than 5%. Yet this concentrated distribution resulted from allocating the stock as evenly as possible. Concentration seems to be a natural outcome of successful employee ownership. One way to have a more uniform allocation would be to stop giving stock bonuses to employees who already have much stock. The only other way to have a much more uniform distribution would be if there was much less growth, but this would mean fewer jobs, a lower stock price, and a generally stagnant company.

This exercise illustrates that stock concentrations are a natural outcome of successful employee ownership. Our employees will

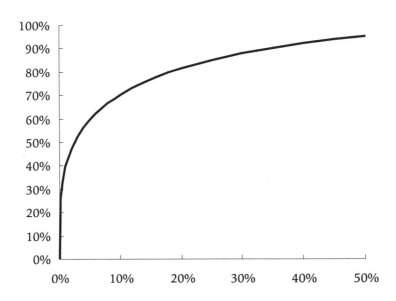

Figure 9-2. Cumulative distribution of the stock from the even model where growth is 15% per year and the bonus rate is 4% per year.

have to learn how to deal with the envy and perception of unfairness that these concentrations evoke. Figure 9-1 shows that today's new employees can become the large shareholders of figure 9-2 if they can work long enough and the company can continue its growth. The real motivational magic and change to ownership attitudes seem to occur between years 5 and 15 when the equity values of figure 9-1 begin to accumulate.

Building a Sense of Ownership

Employees at some companies have a strong culture of building shareholder value, even though the actual employee ownership may be less than 10%. Other companies have actually shared substantial equity with their employees with little or no success at changing employee attitudes into an ownership environment. The National Center for Employee Ownership (NCEO) has written extensively[6] that employee participation is the key, and this agrees with my experience. SAIC has a system of committees that address long-term corporate issues at all levels. The Technical Environment Committee is the nonmanagement, grass-roots group. It works hard to assure that all employees are aware of the issues and have the opportunity to have a say in the process. Employee owners do not like to be surprised by sudden, high-level decisions that affect their workplace. On the other hand, difficult decisions can be widely accepted when all have considered the issues and had the chance to have a say.

Joseph Blasi states this in much stronger terms:

> All levels of management must feel that they have a clear shot at a say in any forum of the company from the most grass-roots team to the board room when an activity of the company is not performing well. This is obviously important for any money-making business, but it is doubly important for one where deferring income into employee stock ownership is a priority. Why is this the case? Because managers and employees are at greater risk in such a company. Their wealth is concentrated in one stock or security. The rule of capitalist corporations is that the more equity an investor risks, they are entitled to more involvement in governance. [7]

A particular challenge is to try to give everyone the opportunity to have a say in the process, without misleading anyone that they have the final say. The committee process is necessarily time-consuming and frustrating, so that it is only useful for the long lead time issues. I think of it as tight-loose management. Time-critical decisions must be made quickly and enforced at the appropriate management level. Long-term issues are evolved through committees, soliciting input from many. Participation decisions are quite often better solutions than what line management would conceive, and a broad buy-in by most employees is much more easily achieved. The payoff of participation is a sense of ownership and employees who are more than willing to go the extra mile to build their company.

The final element of a successful employee ownership culture must be the leadership and commitment of top management. Whittlesey demonstrates that some leaders are able to construct a substantial ownership culture with only 10% employee ownership while others flounder hopelessly even with 100% employee ownership.[8] It is particularly difficult for new employees with only minimal stock to embrace employee ownership as described by long-term employees whose holdings are substantial. It clearly takes effective leadership and presentation skills to communicate these ownership ideas to such a skeptical audience.

Conclusion

The three elements of generating an employee ownership culture are participation, leadership, and effective stock flows. I invite you to invent your own methods of leadership and participation that best fit your corporate environment. Which of the stock flows contribute the most to this sense of ownership? When an employee voluntarily pays full price to buy and hold some stock, then you can be most sure of an ownership attitude. Therefore, I am partial to programs that require the employee to write a check or have a payroll deduction, which then may be matched with further stock or options. The decision to invest one's own money seems to be a big step in moving towards developing an ownership attitude.

Stock bonuses and options based on performance will improve performance and will build ownership attitudes, especially if the employee decides to hold rather than sell. Voluntary retirement choices into stock are also effective. Even though company-directed retirement fund stock contributions may be the least effective, any employee ownership is better than no employee ownership.

Would SAIC's stock structure work for traditional, mature, smaller, low-growth companies? Well, it certainly worked for SAIC when it was smaller, and it isn't small anymore. "Mature" and "low-growth" may imply owners who are satisfied living off the profits of the firm. If the owners don't want to reinvest for growth, they likely wouldn't want to dilute their ownership. If they also prefer to increase profits by raising prices or cutting expenses, this is not going to be an employee-friendly firm. On the other hand, there is nothing to prevent such a company from changing its attitudes to one of striving for growth by reinvesting and/or diversifying and sharing its equity with its employees. SAIC's attitude is that we would prefer to own a smaller piece of a bigger pie.

SAIC's question for the future is whether we can continue this growth. You have seen that we have a large set of stock programs that provide the equity flows to those causing the new growth. We design these programs to foster the attitudes of ownership, and we use leadership and extensive participation to help our employees to develop a more true sense of ownership. Quality people are attracted to this environment. Because of this, we believe that we will always be able to outperform any of our competitors who are unwilling to use their equity as productively as we do. We expect to be able to turn this improved performance into continued growth.

Notes

1. J.R. Beyster, "Principles and Practices," *SAIC Employee Handbook* (SAIC, 1984).

2. Fred E. Whittlesey, "Lessons in Employee Ownership: The Airline Industry," *ACA Journal*, winter 1995: 22.

3. Joseph Blasi, "How to Destroy Employee Ownership? How to Keep It?" Talk on employee ownership to Science Applications International Corporation, November 1, 1995.

4. Jane Bryant Quinn, "The Fables of ESOP," *Newsweek*, November 12, 1979.

5. Harry M. Markowitz, *Portfolio Selection: Efficient Diversification of Investments* (New York: John Wiley and Sons, 1959; Yale University Press, 1972).

6. Karen M. Young, Corey Rosen, and Edward J. Carberry, *Theory O: Creating an Ownership Style of Management*, 3rd ed. (Oakland, CA: National Center for Employee Ownership, 1996).

7. Blasi, "How to Destroy Employee Ownership? How to Keep It?"

8. Whittlesey, "Lessons in Employee Ownership," 23.

10

Incentive Programs in a Professional Services Firm

Darryl Orr

In 1993, Smith & Company was barely breaking even. It was a solid firm with a reputation for doing superior work. It paid competitive wages and offered many benefits. The firm was by no means a failure, but it was not generating significant profits. After 30 years, Samuel H. Smith, the principal owner, was growing weary of carrying most of the load.

Things began to turn around in 1994. With the establishment of an employee stock ownership plan (ESOP) and adoption of open-book management, profits have soared. The value of the business has more than doubled. Employment has increased from 24 to 35. Total employment is predicted to reach 50 people within the next three years. A new office addition has been completed. A five-year ESOP loan was paid off in two years and more stock has been purchased from Smith. The employee owners are learning about business—*their* business—and it shows. The company's finances have dramatically improved. Smith is making more money (as are the employees). More importantly, he's having more fun.

The Firm

Smith & Company, located in southeast Missouri, is a medium-size professional firm that provides civil engineering, surveying, and testing services to public and private clients. The firm, founded in 1965, employs 35 people. Smith & Company engineers design bridges, highways, airports, water systems, wastewater systems, and drainage facilities. Its surveyors perform site surveys for architects and other engineering firms, construction contractors, government agencies, and individual property owners. The testing department provides quality control on projects designed by other architectural and engineering firms as well as on Smith & Company projects. Employees' educational credentials range from high school diplomas to master's degrees in business administration or engineering. Some employees are salaried; others are hourly workers.

The Smith & Company ESOP

In 1993 the firm's principal owner, Sam Smith, decided to begin selling his stock. For several reasons, he picked an employee stock ownership plan (ESOP) to accomplish this goal. First, he could sell his stock with maximum financial and tax advantages. Second, rather than divest himself of all stock immediately, he could sell portions of stock to coincide with his plans for retirement (which was still several years in the future). Third, he could sell his stock to his own employees. After all, they, or employees like them, had helped him stay in business for 30 years.

In 1994, Smith established the ESOP and used it to borrow enough money to buy 30% of the company with a five-year note. The ESOP is conventionally structured, with stock allocation based on salary and with graduated vesting starting at 20% after three years of employment and increasing to 100% after seven years.

The basic premise behind an ESOP is that if each employee owns a part of the firm, then each employee will be motivated to make that firm thrive. When people put their money into other companies, it is an *investment*. When they own a piece of the firm where they work, it is a *commitment*.

For an ESOP to be truly successful, it is not enough to call each employee an "owner"; each employee must think of himself or herself as an owner. Commitment to the spirit of the ESOP must come from the top. Employees will think of themselves as owners only when "the Boss" thinks of them as owners. In many firms, the question is not whether or not the employees are ready for an ESOP; the question is whether or not "the Boss" is ready for an ESOP. The three main ingredients needed to instill that thinking in both parties are education, communication, and dedication.

Senior management must be dedicated to educating all employee owners by communicating all of the information needed to successfully run *their* business. To that end, Smith implemented several incentive programs, both monetary and nonmonetary, to motivate his people to increase the firm's success and to begin the educational process of changing attitudes from those of being "hired hands" to those of being "owners."

Open-Book Management and Education Programs

Open-book management is defined in Dr. Arthur R. Pell's book, *The Complete Idiot's Guide to Managing People*, as "a management style in which employees are considered full partners in the operation of a business. One characteristic of this management style is that employees have a direct stake in their company's success (if the business is profitable, they share in the profits; if not, there are no profits to share). Another characteristic is that every employee has access to numbers that are critical to tracking the company's performance and are given the training and tools to understand them."

It sounds relatively simple, doesn't it? Well, it isn't!

No conscientious parent would hand a child a set of car keys without instruction and practice on the technique of driving, at least not if the parent wanted the child *and the car* to return home safely. Likewise, managers cannot hand the "keys" of the company over to employees unskilled in business. Education must come first. As employees become more and more proficient in ownership, more and more responsibility can and should be turned over to them.

Any worthwhile endeavor, especially education, requires real effort, persistence, skill, and leadership. Management cannot just throw a monthly financial statement out on the table in front of the employees and say, "Here's the open book, think like owners." Opening the books is the easy part; teaching everyone to understand those books and the business is much more difficult.

Installing the ESOP at Smith & Company went smoothly. The next step, making ownership part of our corporate thinking, was more difficult, even painful to some. Change scares many people. According to Kenneth Blanchard, author of *The One Minute Manager* and several other books, when people are asked to do something different, they focus on what they have to give up, not on what they are going to gain. People have several concerns when asked to change. Their first concern is for *information:* What do you have in mind? Am I free to ask questions? The second concern is *personal:* What is going to happen to me? Will I survive this change? The third concern is *implementation:* How is the change going to be done? The fourth concern is *impact:* What will this change cost financially and emotionally? What is the benefit?

Some employees, including one senior manager, left the firm. Some had grown comfortable with the "old way of doing things." Some said that they wanted to concentrate on their job, not the business; they could not understand or accept that the two were inseparable. The daily scorecard distributed to everyone in the company showed who was hitting their billable target and who was not. Some did not like having their productivity, or lack of it, measured.

Little is written about the people who do not want the responsibility of ownership; however, every firm has some of those people. Some people develop an ownership mentality slower than others; some never do. Many times, they are excellent workers and are an asset to the firm in every other way. They cannot and should not be written off or dismissed. They have their place in an open-book management firm, although they will miss out on a lot of fun. Sadly, some good people move on to other firms and a different vision. On the positive side, some not-so-good people leave as well.

Weekly Management and Department Meetings

To begin the educational process, Smith started meeting weekly with managers to discuss business and ESOP issues. These managers then met weekly with their departments to relay the information to all employees. These meetings continue and are vital to getting the word out and keeping everyone involved in the day-to-day business at Smith & Company.

Monthly Company Meetings

Each month a company-wide meeting is held to discuss business. Topics may include finances, marketing, new projects, possible projects, five-year growth projections, department head reports, committee reports, and anything else people want to cover. Although participation is voluntary, attendance is generally 100%.

Monthly Financial Meetings

Just a day or two before each monthly company meeting, when the financial statements are received from our outside accounting firm, voluntary Tuesday and Wednesday evening meetings are conducted to review finances. About 60 to 75% of the employees attend these financial meetings.

At first, Smith conducted these financial meetings himself. In his words, that approach had "zero credibility," which hurt; some of those skeptical employees had worked with him for a long time. He knew he was being honest and was giving the employees a true picture of the company's finances. But rather than dwell on the skepticism, he moved ahead by assigning five people at random to study the financial statements. They met with the firm's outside CPA and then picked one person to make the presentation at the next company meeting. The financials got credibility. Now different volunteers make the presentations at each of the two monthly financial meetings.

In addition to increased credibility, letting various people give the financial presentations helps more people learn the financials well enough to explain them to others. Before you can teach a subject well, you first have to learn it. More of our people are made a part of the process; their business education is advanced.

Advantages: People learn about business; specifically, they learn about *their* business. People learn that what they do affects the "bottom line"; they become financially responsible.

Disadvantages: Numbers are boring, boring, boring to some people. CPAs have their own language, a language that many people find utterly foreign and confusing, with terms such as "assets and liabilities," "stock equity," "accounts receivable," and "accumulated depreciation." People tend not to trust things they do not understand. It takes effort, skill, and time to make financial presentations interesting and credible. It also takes a lot of patience.

The Balanced Daily Scorecard

According to a recent review in the August 19, 1996, issue of *Open-Book Management Bulletin,* published by Open-Book Management, Inc., authors Robert S. Kaplan and David P. Norton assert in their new book, *The Balanced Scorecard* (Boston: Harvard Business School Press, 1996), that companies need a variety of measures to monitor their success. A company must focus on numbers that "translate a business unit's mission and strategy into tangible objectives and measures." Financial objectives must be linked to strategic goals, such as expanding your customer base by 20%. A *balanced scorecard* is essential in ensuring that financial goals have a business rationale.

According to Kaplan and Norton, financial targets must be linked to what they call "performance drivers." External performance drivers include such measures as customer satisfaction, customer retention, new-customer acquisition, and customer profitability. Internal performance drivers focus on business processes and measure quality, delivery time, and labor productivity. Drivers can be long-term or short-term. Simply put, external drivers concentrate on the customer; internal drivers concentrate on the employee. A successful company must concentrate on both. To keep the customer happy you must keep the employee happy. Focusing exclusively on financial returns leads to oblivion.

Certain key numbers—in the case of professional services firms, *billable hours*—will move the bottom line in the right direction. Employees need to understand the link between profit/loss and billable hours. Everyone, managers and employees, must understand that it is not enough to have high billable rates; the work must also be completed within budget and on time. In other words, employees must not just bill time to a project; they must complete the project. Managers and employees must track each project assigned to them to assure that it gets "out the door" on time and within the fee.

To reach our profit goals, we must bill the hours; however, to keep the customer happy (and earn future profits), we must satisfy the customer's needs by delivering a good quality product on time and within budget.

Incentive Programs and the Great Game of Business

The Great Game of Business

To survive, a business must do two things: (1) make money and (2) generate cash. Everything else is a means to that end. Smith was introduced to this simple concept in 1993 at a "Great Game of Business" ("Great Game") seminar conducted by representatives of Springfield ReManufacturing Corporation (SRC) in Springfield, Missouri. He had been steered in SRC's direction when attending an ESOP seminar earlier that year in Memphis, Tennessee.

After returning from that Great Game seminar, Smith began to plant the seeds of the Great Game at Smith & Company. Smith bought copies of Jack Stack's book *The Great Game of Business* and distributed them to his managers. After reading it, Smith and his managers discussed how to introduce the Great Game to the other employees. In the beginning the games were modest.

Smith & Company, like most professional service firms, makes its money selling its billable hours. Time sheets were turned in daily, although some people would fall two or three days behind. In 1993, billable hours were not as high as we felt they could be;

the firm was barely breaking even. We needed a game that would increase our billable hours. Obviously, this would increase our income and consequently our profit. Our first game was set up before our ESOP, but we really started getting into the games after the ESOP. The games help us *understand* the business; the ESOP helps us *think* like business owners.

Setting up the game was crucial; it would mean the difference between the game being the *management's* game or the *employees'* game. Anything perceived to be the management's game would probably be doomed to failure. Thus, every employee was involved in the process. Every employee was asked: How many billable hours per week did he or she think were reasonable for him or her to achieve? After input from each employee, the billable hours "target" of each employee was then multiplied by that employee's hourly billable rate. Then, based on everyone's individual target, the billable income of every employee was totaled to determine the firm's monthly billable income. We had our first goal; hit that total monthly billable income and everybody would get a bonus.

That first month—December 1993—we played for a bonus of $100 per person. Each day the billable hours and billable income for each employee were tabulated on a chart—our *scorecard*. The scorecard was passed out to every employee every day. Everyone knew where they, and the company, stood. The increase in billable hours was immediate, even beyond what people said they could do. We made our first goal; we got our $100. We had stopped the decline; profit was headed up. Some people started thinking that there just might be something to this Great Game of Business.

The Bigger Bucket of Bucks Game

We do not ignore monetary rewards. In fact, we love to give away money to ourselves—as long as it comes from our profits. We've played for "Bucks" and "Buckets of Bucks." We are now playing for "Bigger Buckets of Bucks." In 1994 we hit our annual goal by the end of the third quarter and distributed $50,000 in bonuses. In 1995, $77,500 was handed out. Five buckets had been budgeted in 1996; however, adding a second floor and eight offices to our building and installing a computer network decreased productivity. Even so, three profit goals (buckets) were met in 1996 and $42,500 was distributed in bonuses. The new building addition and the computer network have helped us to increase productivity substantially this year; we are back on track.

Our main monetary game—Bigger Bucket of Bucks—is based on profit goals (six buckets) that are set at the beginning of the year. When we reach a preset profit (fill a bucket), as determined by monthly financial reports prepared by our accounting firm, a portion of that profit is distributed to each employee based on salary. We make that a big deal. The bonus is handed out to each employee at our monthly company meeting, and then we celebrate our success with a cookout. Sometimes caps or jackets or T-shirts with the company logo are handed out to everyone to underscore the achievement. Company photographs are taken; sometimes the press is invited. We want people, including our clients, to know that we are a successful employee-owned company. Up to now, profit goals have been set by senior management. However, during the preparation of the annual budget, each department head and each of the company's six committees are asked to contribute their estimates of the next year's expenses and income. As the employee-owners' business knowledge increases, so does their involvement in budget preparation and game development.

Advantages: Monetary games keep our people interested in the "bottom line." Open-book management and the ESOP are based on everyone's sharing in the success or failure of the company. When the firm is profitable, bonuses keep that promise.

Disadvantages: It can be argued that money alone can be more of a de-motivator than a motivator. There is more to the success of a company than profits. Concentrating only on the bottom line can lead to substandard work, unhappy customers, and disgruntled employees. An unhappy company is not a successful company no matter how much money it makes. Of course, it should also be pointed out that a company that is losing money is more likely to have disgruntled employees producing substandard work that leads to unhappy customers.

The Accounts Receivable Game

Games are used to target and solve specific problems. For example, our company had an accounts receivable (A/R) problem. We were making money (profits were up), but we weren't generating cash. Our A/R (money owed us) exceeded 20% of our total annual billings. On paper, we were doing great. We were making money, but every now and then Smith still had to call our banker to borrow money to make the payroll. We had to pay interest on that borrowed money, interest that came out of our profits.

Everyone connected to billing—engineers, managers, department heads, and bookkeeper—was gathered together. Smith explained the problem very simply: the firm needed cash. The group was divided into five teams; each team was given a list of past-due accounts that were outstanding for at least 30 days. Special emphasis was placed on collecting those overdue accounts. The mission was to reduce the accounts receivable to 15% of our total annual billings and keep it there for three months. If they were successful, each team member would get $100 cash.

Some collections were as simple as making a phone call; some took a letter or the resubmittal of the invoice. Some required meeting with the client to resolve a misunderstanding. Slowly but surely, the A/R is decreasing; we are generating cash. We will pay out $1,700 in bonuses but save $6,000 in interest. Another lesson in business will be learned.

Advantages: It teaches our people that it is just as important to generate cash as it is to make money. It makes everyone, not just Smith and the bookkeeper, responsible for and interested in collecting the money due us.

Disadvantages: Many people hate to collect money; they feel that it burdens them with a very unpleasant task. It can take engineers and managers away from "billable" work, which decreases productivity. A "Catch 22" is that the more successful a firm is at billing its time, the more A/R it generates and a certain portion of that increased A/R will become overdue. It seems to be easier to make money than to generate cash; however, it is easier to generate cash when you are making money than when you are losing it.

Nonmonetary Incentive Programs

The monetary incentive programs are not so much designed to inspire our people as they are to keep people interested in the business. In fact, money alone is not usually a very good motivator in the long run. The key to inspiring people is not throwing money at them; it is throwing appreciation at them. Another key is providing a structure, an opportunity, that allows people to do a very good job. People are *interested* in making money but people are *inspired* by such things as opportunity and knowing that they are successful and being recognized for a job well done. The best incentive programs provide those things.

At Smith & Company, we look for reasons to celebrate. Engineering is a serious business; lots of money, even lives, can hang in the balance. Our people work hard. The work demands concentration and attention to detail; therefore, to prevent burnout, our people need to unwind from time to time. We invent "Little Games" toward that end. For example, we may set a *daily billable income* target; when we hit it, the department heads cook breakfast for everyone. Get people together; have fun! Remember, it's called the Great *Game* of Business.

Our games are also designed to encourage teamwork by concentrating on company-wide goals. Everyone must be involved in the business to make it a success. The company is only as strong as its weakest link; every job, every function, every employee is critical to that strength. Everyone has to realize that we sink or swim together.

Most people want to be challenged. Incentive programs should be designed to encourage high performance. Successful companies are not made up of average employees. Time after time, our people have set goals for themselves that even management thought were unattainable. Time after time, management has been proven wrong. An $8,000 billable day was set as a goal; we hit it! Then an $8,500 day; we hit it! A $9,000 day; a $10,000 day; a $40,000 week; a $45,000 week; we hit them all. It seems that the sky is the limit. Sometimes, the best thing a manager can do is just get out of the way and let a person do his or her job.

Keep the games simple. Do not try to solve all of your company's problems with one game. Keep in mind that the size of the prize is not important; it is showing appreciation for a job well done that motivates people. A good memory lasts longer than cash.

Advantages: People are kept interested in the business. Problems are solved. The games can be challenging and still be fun. They can be used to improve morale and foster teamwork.

Disadvantages: It takes time and effort to administrate the games. New games are demanded after the completion of the old ones. Employee owners will challenge you to challenge them. Sometimes having fun is hard work.

Work Teams

Each employee serves on one or more work teams of his or her choice. Team members gather at luncheon meetings—most of the time the lunch is paid for by the firm—to discuss their team's function, such as long-range planning, outside activities, the building and grounds, computers and office equipment, and vehicles and field equipment. We have a team looking into areas for the firm to expand or diversify into (some of the golfers want to open a golf pro shop). The work teams make their recommendations to the management staff at one of the weekly meetings. They are expected to present costs of implementation as well as the pros and cons of their recommendation. Each recommendation is carefully considered, and if the idea seems feasible, it is introduced to all employees for further discussion at our monthly company meeting.

All work team recommendations are taken seriously. They are discussed and sound reasons are given if an idea cannot be implemented. The intent is to allow all employees to have a say in the direction that the company takes.

Advantages: More people are involved in the running of the company. Management has a larger pool from which to draw good ideas. People learn that implementing an idea or program, even an excellent one, requires money, time, and effort. They learn that due to the cost or some other valid reason, not every idea or program can be implemented. It helps them understand that in business, as in life, there are consequences that must be considered before action can be taken.

Disadvantages: Work team members may put a lot of time and effort into ideas that cannot be implemented. This can lead to disappointment and, if not handled correctly by management, to the feeling that the teams are merely window dressing and that the employees are not thought of as "real" owners. Sometimes a work team might develop a vested interest in keeping the team intact even after its mission has been completed. If so, the team is in danger of becoming a committee; committees tend to turn into bureaucracies.

Opening the Books Wider

Almost 80% of our people have computers on their desks. Because we are networked, every person is able to tap into the company's bookkeeping program; this means that almost every employee has access to the day-to-day finances of the company. With a few keystrokes, a person can find out how much money was taken in that day or how much money was spent. They know how much time has been spent on every ongoing project and how much fee remains. They have access to information that is available only to a select few in most firms. Communication is easier, which has led to increased interest in the business.

The Future

We start planning for the next year around the middle of the present year. With everyone involved, a new budget is prepared and more new games and different incentive programs are designed. We want games and programs to encourage improved performance by rewarding such improvements. They should encourage learning more about our business by focusing attention on the right numbers.

We hope to initiate individual incentive programs, peer-recognition award programs, bigger and better bonus plans, and family recognition programs—all designed by our employee owners.

Individual Incentive Programs

At Smith & Company, managers are encouraged to informally recognize and express appreciation to individuals for outstanding achievement; however, to date we have avoided emphasis on "official" individual incentive programs. It is very hard to overcome the "us against them" attitude that tends to occur in any company. For example, there may be feelings of "hourly versus salaried" or "surveyors versus engineers" or "managers versus employees."

Some of us are concerned that by rewarding individuals or departments, we will destroy the teamwork that is necessary to accomplish our company-wide goals. However, we also realize that even in a company where almost everyone is involved in the business, there are individuals who contribute more than their fair share. They work longer or harder or more efficiently than other employees. If a firm truly wants people to be better than average, then it must find a way to encourage better-than-average performance. You receive the type of performance that you reward. Treating everyone the same encourages mediocrity.

The danger of formal individual recognition programs is that one person or department might be set against another. After all, when one person "wins" an individual award, that means all other employees have "lost" that award. If cutthroat competition results, teamwork will go out the window. There is also the danger that individuals or departments will be conditioned to narrowly focus on their own success at the expense of the company. The system might become "political" or become a personality-over-substance contest. To avoid that, our first step will be to recruit a team made up of a representative cross-section of our employees to come up with an individual incentive program. Any acceptable incentive program must balance individual incentives with company-wide incentives. It must promote cooperative effort.

We feel that the employee team might be able to develop a program that is more likely to be considered fair by all employees than if the program was developed by senior management. That means faster buy-in to that program and greater chance of success without resulting in the "us against them" attitude. We intend to proceed with great caution.

Peer-Recognition Award Program

Soon, a formal award program will be implemented that will honor employees who show a positive attitude or go "above and beyond the call of duty" to help a client or someone else within the firm. The nominations will come from co-workers who witness the outstanding efforts. The company will even have an award program for the employee who comes up with a catchy name for this peer-recognition program.

Bigger and Better Bonus Programs

In the past, our bonuses have been based on salary. For example, each person got 10% of his or her salary; therefore, the higher the salary, the bigger the bonus. Some lesser-paid employees feel cheated because their bonuses are smaller. As a consequence, for some people the positive impact of the bonus is lessened; their motivation to succeed is decreased.

To rectify that problem, a new bonus plan is needed. All employees are being encouraged to submit ideas for new and improved bonus plans. One plan under consideration is to pay out 25% of the bonus pool in equal shares and 75% based on salary. Whatever the bonus plan, it must accomplish three things: (1) motivate people, (2) help them learn the business, and (3) focus attention on the right numbers.

Family Recognition Programs

It is common in a professional services firm to request that an employee work extra hours to complete an important project or to attend a client's after-hours meeting or attend an overnight conference. While that employee's sacrifice is sometimes recognized by management, the sacrifice of his or her family goes unrecognized. The missed dinners, the missed birthday parties, the missed ball games, and so on all add up. Without the support of the family, it is very difficult for an employee to continue making that extra effort.

We intend to develop a program to recognize the sacrifice made by an employee's family. It might be something as simple as writing a note to the employee's family thanking them for support, acknowledging the good work their family member has done, and explaining the importance of the project to the company. Perhaps the employee and his or her family will be given a gift certificate for dinner in a nice restaurant or maybe even an all-expense-paid weekend retreat for the family. The size or type of gift is relatively unimportant; what is important is that the sacrifice be recognized by the company.

Conclusion

An ESOP gives the company to the employees; open-book management gives them the information needed to run it; incentive and education programs teach them to be successful. One will not work without the others. Education takes communication and dedication by everyone.

The process of going from "employee" to "owner" is slow and at times even painful. The education process must never end. Installing an ESOP and adopting open-book management does not eliminate a firm's day-to-day problems. It does not eliminate the need for managing your company or its employees. But opening the books does make management easier in many respects by changing the attitude of employees. When your employees become your partners, the workload and responsibility are spread around. You are no longer solely responsible for the success of the company.

When everyone shares in the company's future, whether good or bad, it does not take long for people to see that they will reap benefits when the future is good. In fact, employee owners will work very hard to make that future good. Smith & Company's experience with an ESOP and open-book management proves it.

Recommended Reading

Scott Adams, *The Dilbert Principle* (New York: Harper Business, 1996).

Kenneth Blanchard and Spencer Johnson, *The One Minute Manager* (Berkley Books, 1981).

John Case, *Open-Book Management: The Coming Business Revolution* (New York: Harper Business, 1995).

Bob Nelson, *1001 Ways to Reward Employees* (New York: Workman Publishing, 1994).

Dr. Arthur R. Pell, *The Complete Idiot's Guide to Managing People* (Alpha Books, 1995).

John Schuster, Jill Carpenter, and Patricia Kane, *The Power of Open-Book Management* (New York: John Wiley & Sons, 1996).

Jack Stack, *The Great Game of Business* (New York: Currency Books, 1992).

Karen M. Young, Corey Rosen, and Edward J. Carberry, *Theory O: Creating an Ownership Style of Management*, 3rd ed. (Oakland, CA: National Center for Employee Ownership, 1996).

Using the Scanlon Plan in an ESOP Company

Bill Nicholson and Neil N. Koenig

Employee stock ownership plan (ESOP) companies understandably encourage pride of ownership. Initially, the emphasis is on the employees' equity stake in the company: "We're employee owners!" This is usually followed by management efforts to instill job ownership: "We do our jobs as if we owned them!" The payoff for this ownership is typically in the future—a handsome retirement fund exceeding the norm of non-ESOP retirees, assuming the ESOP company is successful in the long run.

There are a couple of problems with the deferred nature of the ESOP benefit, however. The first is that between now and retirement, employees have urgent day-to-day financial needs, and companies in today's economy cannot afford high labor costs. Market competition and international competitors' low wages have made the yearly pay raise a thing of the past. So how do companies keep costs down and still reward their employees?

The other problem with the deferred nature of the ESOP benefit is that it often is of little help with the challenge of motivating employees on a day-to-day basis. For all but the small percentage who are truly self-motivated, something more is needed than the expected biweekly paycheck and a rare remark of recognition. This is especially critical now when the routine day-to-day work is more demanding and exacting than anything most employees have ever done in their lives. Pep talks, piecework, preaching, and pizzas have all been tried and found wanting. So how do we motivate the employees who require external motivators (the majority, we fear) as conditions created by the economy and competitors demand more and more of them?

What Companies Are Looking For

Companies have long looked for ways to reward and encourage worker commitment. Additionally, companies today are looking for ways to avoid reinforcing the entitlement mentality. What we all seek are ways to provide immediate, tangible rewards based on merit. Merit means the reward is earned—truly earned. Rewards should be given for results, quality linked to quantity, effort teamed with smarts, and ideas translated into customer service.

In addition, companies want to discourage internal and individual competition that siphons off energy and effort on behalf of the whole. What is key is rewarding work that contributes to the whole: "We compete with other companies, not with each other. In here we work together if we want to win."

Companies today seek a group incentive plan based on results achieved by all working together for the entire company. The reward must be tangible, in the form of real money. And the reward must be frequent; a reward delayed is a reward forgotten.

A Partnership Approach to Group Incentive Plans

The compelling, simple logic of ESOPs is the partnership among all groups within the company. ESOPs need to be run as partnerships between management and front-line workers, operations and sales, manufacturing and marketing, veterans and newcomers, men and women: "We're all partners in this. That's how we succeed." Establishing a group incentive plan is the perfect opportunity for an ESOP company to prove its partnership approach to doing business.

Incentive plans are no place to practice top-down management. To do so is to revert to traditional parent-child paternalistic condescension: "If you eat your vegetables we'll increase your allowance." As with anything, it is best to make people insiders regarding a group incentive plan. This is especially true when it comes to money, let alone money for which employees must work hard while wages and full employment are held in check.

Incentive plans work best when everyone has bought in on the plan and in effect "owns" the plan. This means that management and front-line workers must participate together in selecting an appropriate group bonus plan. This requires an educational effort concerning the economic, business, market, and financial realities facing the company, as well as education about group incentive plans. The goal, after all, is to have everyone capable of thinking, deciding, and acting as businesspersons. This educational effort is best done both in person and in writing.

The first step is to sell the idea of a group incentive plan. Groups no larger than 30 or so employees from across the company should meet with executive leaders for crisp, clear presentations about the big-picture realities and the possibilities afforded by a group incentive plan. A genuine question-and-answer period must be part of these sessions.

The second step is to establish a recommendation committee. Ideally it would be comprised of one senior leader, two middle or supervisory managers, and four front-line partners, each peer group selecting its own representatives. Any appearance that the group incentive plan idea itself or the best plan for the company is a management gimmick or fad or ploy of the company to get more out of its employees for nothing will doom the effort. Here is where the ESOP partnership referred above serves as a role model. The committee is authorized to study, select, and present the best and most appropriate options to the company.

The third step is to reconvene the larger groups as in step one. Members of the recommendation committee present the options, including their opinion of what the most favorable option is. Each option's pros and cons are outlined. Each option is examined for how it would work and what it would mean in real money earned.

Emphasis is also needed on what now would be required of everyone—from ideas for increased productivity, cost cutting, and increased efficiencies to greater cooperation and multidisciplined approaches to solving and preventing problems. Time for genuine questions and answers is critical, as are handouts that clearly and easily spell out the contents of the presentation of the recommendation committee.

The fourth and final step is selection across the company. This can be done by individual voting or by group consensus in small meetings conducted by members of the recommendation committee.

The entire process, from step one through step four, should take no longer than a month. Any longer and momentum is lost. Any less and skepticism is engendered: "They're trying to push something down our throats again."

It is best to treat the adoption of a group incentive plan as a year-long experiment. The speed of change in today's business world requires continual evaluation and improvement anyway. And twelve monthly results should even out seasonal variables. A one-year commitment also shows confidence and courage: "As partners we can make a difference in the year ahead. And we'll reward ourselves as we go along. We can do it!"

The Distribution Company and Its $9.75 Experiment

An American distributor of building materials (the company wishes to remain anonymous) has benefited from a group incentive plan since 1975. It has 200 employees, is 100% ESOP owned, is an industry leader, and is strong financially in the cycle-sensitive world of residential and commercial construction. The company considers its management style to be participative and encourages employee involvement in the business. This is done in both structured and unstructured meetings, regular work group meetings, ad-hoc problem-solving meetings, and frequent lunch meetings with executive leaders. Leaders have dubbed the latter give-and-take meetings as "LBEL"—Leadership By Eating Lunch.

The management of the company made a conscious decision to be more participative in the early 1970s in response to an unsuccessful effort by front-line workers to unionize. A planning session that included all plant employees resulted. The number-one issue identified at this pivotal meeting was the desire for an incentive plan.

A committee of employees was drawn from both the shop floor and the administrative offices. It considered the possibilities for an incentive plan, coming up with three alternatives. The first was piecework, which is hard to measure in the distribution business and has the tendency to overemphasize individual competition. The second alternative was profit sharing; the committee's objection here was the difficulty of controlling the payoff.

The best fit for the company, the committee concluded, was a group incentive plan. They discovered the Scanlon Plan, dating from the early 1930s, in Douglas MacGregor's classic, *The Human Side of Enterprise*, published in 1960. Research in the local library turned up an article on the Parker Pen Company's use of the Scanlon Plan. Parker Pen was contacted. It identified its consultant as Fred Lesieur, who happened to have been an associate of the late Joseph Scanlon. Lesieur felt there was no need to get together: "Just read my book" (Fred G. Lesieur, *The Scanlon Plan: A Frontier in Labor-Management Cooperation* [Cambridge: MIT Press, 1958]). He sent his book for $8.00. The phone call cost $1.75. From this $9.75 investment the distributor worked out its own simplified version of the Scanlon Plan, implementing it on January 1, 1975. The company was proud to proceed without expensive outside consultants, going forward with employee participants practicing partnership—this in the wake of the recent union threat.

The Adapted Scanlon Plan

The distributor discovered as it studied the Scanlon Plan that it is more than an incentive formula. It should be looked at as a system of management because it involves a formal feedback system. Rather than adopting the Plan indiscriminately, it added the Plan's feedback system to its own management system, continuing to emphasize especially the participative, partnership approach to running the company.

The company's plan rewards productivity as a function of the interplay between labor costs (payroll) and current sales. Current sales were chosen because turnaround time in distributing is so rapid. Thus, the formula in use has been payroll divided by current sales.

The company investigated its performance over the years and calculated its historical standard for payroll as a percentage of sales (12% in the example below). The percentage is set by the employees themselves and is reviewed annually. Hence, incentive payments come from new profits.

The bonus is measured and paid monthly to provide immediate and continuous feedback. The bonus is paid in cash, in checks separate from regular payroll checks. Fifty percent is paid monthly and the other half is retained to cover months when seasonal fluctuations occur. Anything left over at the end of the year is paid as a year-end bonus. Payroll is not leveled for vacations and holidays. New workers must wait 18 months to qualify for participation in the plan. There are monthly and annual reports, in keeping with the financial educational needs of partnership-style management.

To illustrate, let us suppose that annual sales are $1 million and that 12% is the historical standard for payroll as a percentage of sales. That gives an allowed payroll of $120,000 (12% of $1 million). Actual payroll turns out to be $100,000, leaving a $20,000 pool of bonus money to be divided among the employees. The company retains 25% (here, $5,000) and the employees get 75% (here, $15,000). Of this amount to be divided among the employees, half is paid out immediately (here, $7,500) and the other half is placed in a reserve account for the rainy-day months and, if anything is left, the year-end bonus (table 11-1).

Variations of Group Incentive Plans

The Scanlon Plan rewards productivity as measured by payroll as a percentage of sales. As the Scanlon Plan has evolved, some companies have modified the original ratio to include additional costs

Table 11-1. How the Scanlon Plan Works at the Distribution Company

Sales	$1,000,000
Historical standard for payroll as % of sales (12%)	× .12
Allowed payroll	120,000
Actual payroll	(100,000)
Bonus pool	20,000
Employee share (75% of bonus pool)	15,000
Reserve account (50%)	(7,500)
Monthly bonus to be paid	$ 7,500

so that participants do not focus on one cost at the expense of another. For example, a person on a grinding machine found that he could improve the payroll-to-sales ratio by tightening the wheel and increasing the speed in the process. While the payroll-to-sales ratio improved, the cost of replacing the grinding wheels increased and total company performance declined. Other companies have included the cost of payroll and damage as a percentage of sales. Sales can be net of customer returns, which includes a customer service focus in the ratio. Some manufacturers have found a ratio of payroll to the sales value of production to be better, as their productivity is related to production, not shipment.

As companies tailor-make their group incentive plans, they must not overlook other costs for short-term gain at the expense of long-term strategies. This requires an environment of ongoing dialogue about the business (e.g., the lunch meetings discussed above) so that people understand how to build the business for long-term success.

A principle of the Scanlon Plan is that the standard of performance is current results. The standard, therefore, has been set by the participants, not an outside resource. Our distributor decided that the best representation of current performance was the average of the last two years. A caution is called for: Some companies have implemented the plan in an economic downturn. Consequently, current performance would be based on unusually low productivity. This would result in productivity bonuses paid before they were warranted, a detriment to the company and therefore to the participants.

Another important principle of the Scanlon Plan is that the ratio is reviewed annually and adjusted for extenuating circumstances. This is the case, for example, when productivity gains are from technology. The intent is to reward participants for gains in *their* productivity, encouraging an environment of working smarter, not harder. Our distributor once changed the ratio during a period of severe economic downturn so that productivity bonuses were not paid while the company was below a break-even point.

Making the Group Incentive Plan Work

At the company we have discussed, the plan is explained to employees as follows: "The plan adjusts the company's pay structure to its ability to pay—if we've got it, we'll pay it; if we don't, we can't and won't." Under the plan, payroll becomes a variable cost. The issue for employees is to choose between fewer people earning more money or more people earning less money. The cost to the company is the same.

Because the plan makes the money paid to workers a variable, sales-driven cost, it allows the company to avoid major work-force cuts when revenues are down. This prevents the company from losing experienced, trained employees, and is a very important advantage both for the company and for the employees who would otherwise be laid off during major downturns. A further advantage is the merit-based reward that is at the heart of this incentive plan. The harder people work, the smarter they work, the more creatively they work, and the more efficiently they work, the more the reward is. Entitlement, politics, and seniority have nothing to do with the reward. The employees themselves must make the incentive pay.

The President/CEO of the distributorship in this discussion related how business in early 1996 was slow, employees becoming "crabby," as he put it—their way of expressing boredom, frustration with not being challenged, and some fear that perhaps the summer would not be busy. "And people were grousing that incentive pay wasn't as it was in the good old days," he added. When business dramatically picked up in July, the President/CEO sent out the following message to every employee:

> Want to earn a 25% bonus this month? It can be done. Let's not lose sight of the fact that WE have to MAKE the incentive pay. Here's how August can be a 25% bonus: Our average invoicing for the last 9 days is $225,000 per day. If we can ship 10% more a day in August, with the same crew and the same hours, the incentive earnings will be 25%—half paid in September and half paid with the year-end bonus.
>
> If we can do that and reduce errors, we don't have to waste money correcting them—and the incentive rises.
>
> How many people do you know that have the opportunity to earn an additional 25% this month? I think the answer is not many. This is the place where that opportunity exists—and if we don't take advantage of it, we will have missed a big chance.

The President/CEO says, "Everyone in the company had this in their hands on August 1. Based on the feedback I've gotten, including feedback at several of our LBEL meetings, this really created some excitement."

By mid-October the President/CEO summarized how their modified Scanlon Plan worked out as a group incentive plan: "We have been at absolute peak for about eight weeks, and we are doing just fine. We have gone from twice a week lunch meetings to twice a month—we wanted to keep track of the company's temperature, but didn't really have time for too many meetings. The refrain still comes up: 'We're at our best when we are busy.' The main problem areas this summer were where we were working too many hours. We were really staffed lean. But it was the employees' decision. So when the September incentive checks came out, the hours didn't seem to be so long after all. We had a lot of tired but happy workers around here. Proud, too. And remember, we had absolutely no help from price increases. In fact, our prices are 1% lower than last year. And we incurred some cost increases as well. Yet we made our merit increases. In spite of how tough the environment is to operate in, our people did great. They deserved their bonus."

Border States Electric Supply Bonus Incentive Program

Tammy J. Miller

Border States Electric Supply (BSE) is the 15th-largest distributor of electrical products in the United States. The company operates 17 branch locations in eight states. BSE's 560 employees own the company. The employee stock ownership plan (ESOP), implemented in 1984, holds 80% of the company stock. The remaining company stock is owned by employees outside the ESOP.

As part of an effort to generate more enthusiasm about employee ownership and to promote a philosophy of continuous improvement, a new bonus program was developed. Through March 31, 1994, before the program was implemented, bonuses paid to employees were totally at the discretion of the board of directors. The bonus incentive program was developed and implemented in July 1994. The program emphasizes that employee owners have a right to know how the company works, have a responsibility to positively affect company operations, and have a right to share in the risks and rewards. The program is still in place, although it was revised effective April 1, 1996. This article will describe the program as it was originally designed and then note the changes made in 1996.

The Original Bonus Program

The original bonus incentive program was designed by Paul Madson, president and CEO, and Tammy Miller, vice president of finance. Introduced in July 1994, the program was structured as follows.

Quarterly Bonus

A "bonus day" is equal to compensation for an eight-hour day. Three bonus days were available to branch employees for meeting their goals at the end of each fiscal quarter as follows:

- One bonus day if the branch attained its quarterly gross profit goal.
- One bonus day if the branch attained its quarterly net profit goal.
- One bonus day if the branch exceeded its net profit goal for the quarter by 10%.

Gross profit is equal to sale revenues minus the cost of goods sold. Net profit is equal to the gross profit less operating expenses, plus other income, and minus other expenses. All goals were measured against the branch budget. If the branch failed to earn a bonus day in a quarter, it could be "made up" the next quarter by meeting year-to-date goals.

Year-End Bonus

At year-end, an unlimited number of bonus days were available if the branch and company exceeded net profit goals as follows:

- One bonus day for each 5% the branch exceeded its net profit goal.
- One bonus day for each 5% the company exceeded its net profit goal.

For example, if at year-end the company exceeded its net profit budget by 30%, each employee would receive six bonus days.

Implementation

A videotape was produced and distributed to each branch. The video outlined the main points of the bonus program. After viewing the video, each employee received a brochure summarizing the program.

Ongoing support of the bonus program was (and still is) generated through open-book management. Around the fifteenth of each month, branch managers receive a financial packet. It includes the branch's financial results of the previous month, a financial education piece, and a "bonus board," which, in graphic form, depicts how well the branch is doing compared to its goals. Monthly staff meetings are held to review the contents of the financial packet, distribute bonus checks, promote financial education, discuss progress toward company goals, and discuss overall company operations.

Integral to the success of the bonus program and open-book management is the financial education section. The financial education piece is developed by the company's vice president of finance or its accounting manager. A copy of the financial education piece is distributed to each employee at the monthly meeting, and the contents are discussed with the group. Some of the topics that have been covered in the monthly financial education pieces include:

- *Reading the income statement* (described cost of goods sold, gross profit, expense categories, etc.).

- *Reading the balance sheet* (explained all asset, liability and equity items).

- *Cash flow* (explained how sales, expenses, accounts receivable, inventory, accounts payable, and capital expenditures affect cash flow).

- *Inventory* (explained inventory performance, including turns and GMROI [gross margin return on investment]).

- *Accounts receivable* (described how accounts receivable are generated, collection problems, and related costs).

- *Stock* (defined what stock is, the difference between public and private companies, employee ownership, and stock valuation).

- *Focus on profitability* (defined what employees can do to improve profitability).

- *Budgets* (outlined the budget process and gave employees the tools to participate in and understand the annual budget process).

- *Benchmarking* (explained benchmarking and compared significant performance measures of BSE branches to industry averages).

Each monthly financial education piece is designed to give employees pertinent financial information that will help them to better understand the business, thus empowering them to make a positive impact on company operations. The financial education may also help employees to better understand their own personal finances.

At the monthly meetings, employees are encouraged to share process improvement and cost-saving ideas. Sometimes employees brainstorm on specific branch problems.

Feedback on the Original Program

In December 1995, employees were surveyed to determine what they liked and disliked about the bonus program. They were also asked how to improve it. Overall, the employees liked the program, but they suggested that one quarterly goal be based on overall company performance, not just branch performance. They also suggested that part of the year-end rewards be based on improvement over the prior year rather than the budget.

The Revised Program

The company classifies sales as "stock" if they are of products stocked in a company warehouse, and "direct" if the product is shipped directly from the manufacturer to the customer. A measure called the "stock gross margin" is calculated as follows:

(Sales – Stock Cost of Goods Sold) ÷ Stock Sales

Consistent with industry trends, the company saw its stock gross margins erode during the fiscal year ending March 31, 1996. Additionally, because of expansion into new markets and rapid sales growth, the company's productivity and profitability declined. Facing negative trends, the company set forth a "Focus on Profitability" for fiscal 1997 with three priorities:

1. Improve stock gross margins by 1%.
2. Improve company net profit before taxes to 1.5% of sales.
3. Improve employee productivity (measured as gross margin per employee).

A revised bonus program was introduced on April 1, 1996. (The company's fiscal year is April 1–March 31). The revised program is consistent with the original program in that three bonus days are available each quarter, with additional bonus days available at year-end. However, the performance measures have changed to support the new company priorities and to incorporate feedback received from employees. The revised program is designed with the expectation that each employee will earn a minimum of 20 bonus days per year. Bonus days are paid within 30 days of the quarter-end and within 60 days of the year-end.

Quarterly Bonus

Three bonus days are available to branch employees for meeting their goals at the end of each fiscal quarter as follows:

- One bonus day if the branch's quarterly stock gross profit percent exceeds its budget.
- One bonus day if the branch's quarterly net profit exceeds its budget.

- One bonus day if the company's quarterly net profit exceeds its budget.

Consistent with the original program, if bonus days for branch or company net profit are missed in one quarter, they can be made up in the next quarter if the year-to-date net profit exceeds the budget.

Year-End Bonus

At year-end, branch employees can earn bonus days as follows:

- Bonus days for each 5% the company exceeds its net profit budget.
- Bonus days for improvement in a branch's net profit over the previous year.
- Bonus days for improvement in a branch's gross margin per employee over previous year.
- Bonus days for a branch's net profit exceeding minimum profitability guidelines.

Under the current program, the board of directors may approve a mid-year discretionary bonus of up to five days, payable in late November.

Eligibility

All employees participate in the bonus program. Under the original program, full-commissioned sales representatives did not participate in the program or the staff meetings. This was definitely a flaw. The sales representatives are a vital part of the operations; they contribute greatly to the success of the company and must support all company programs. The full-commissioned sales representatives are now included in all aspects of the revised program.

Corporate employees participate in a similar program with slightly modified performance measures. Branch managers and corporate managers participate in the quarterly bonus program but do not participate in the year-end bonus program. Instead, each manager has a customized year-end bonus program that rewards accomplishment of specific personal goals.

Conclusion

The bonus incentive program is the tool the company uses to promote a basic understanding of business ownership and the philosophy of continuous improvement. Employees are encouraged to help establish budgets, improve processes, cut expenses, improve margins, and improve profitability. The company's employee owners have a right to company financial information, a responsibility to positively affect company operations, and a right to share in the risks and rewards of the company's business. At all times, every employee knows what it takes to win and what the score is.

About the Editor and Contributors

Editor   Scott Rodrick is an author, editor, desktop publisher, and Web developer at the National Center for Employee Ownership (NCEO). He edits the NCEO's *Journal of Employee Ownership Law and Finance,* in which most of these chapters originally appeared.

Chapter 1   Jerry McAdams is national practice leader, Reward and Recognition Systems, for Watson Wyatt Worldwide.

Chapter 2   Cathy Ivancic is a senior consultant for Ownership Development Inc., which specializes in training and organizational development for firms creating an ownership culture. Ivancic, who is a member of the NCEO's board of directors, is based in Akron, Ohio.

Chapter 3   Jack Stack is president of Springfield ReManufacturing Corporation, an employee-owned engine and engine component remanufacturing company in Missouri.

Chapter 4   Peggy Walkush works in employee owner relations at Science Applications International Corporation (SAIC), in a role she created to generate excitement and enthusiasm about employee ownership among employees. Peggy is also a Senior Fellow of the

Foundation for Enterprise Development, a nonprofit organization that helps foster employee ownership worldwide.

Chapter 5   Arthur S. Meyers is a stockholder in the Boston, Massachusetts, law firm of Hutchins, Wheeler and Dittmar, where he chairs the firm's ERISA and compensation practice.

Chapter 6   Corey Rosen is the executive director of the National Center for Employee Ownership (NCEO).

Chapter 7   Fred E. Whittlesey is the founding principal of Compensation and Performance Management, Inc. (CPM), a management consulting firm based in Newport Beach, California. He helps companies allocate financial capital to human capital through performance-based compensation programs and related performance management processes.

Chapter 8   Paul Davis serves as president of Scanlon Plan Associates (SPA). The SPA is a nonprofit organization that provides networking opportunities for member organizations in North America and serves as a worldwide clearinghouse of Scanlon-related research, thought, and practice.

Chapter 9   William H. Scott is a radiation physicist and assistant vice president at Science Applications International Corporation (SAIC). In addition to conducting radiation shielding research, Scott serves as SAIC's Participation Advocate to improve employee involvement and the understanding of employee ownership.

Chapter 10   Darryl Orr, chief operations officer at Smith & Company, is a registered professional engineer. He has owned and operated consulting engineering firms since 1971.

Chapter 11   Bill Nicholson is a CPA active in the ESOP community. Neil N. Koenig, Ph.D., owns Leadership R&D, a management consulting firm specializing in leadership development, family businesses, and ESOP companies.

Chapter 12   Tammy J. Miller, CPA, is the vice president of finance for Border States Industries, Inc. (Border States Electric Supply).

About the NCEO

The National Center for Employee Ownership (NCEO) is widely considered to be the leading authority in employee ownership in the U.S. and the world. Established in 1981 as a nonprofit information and membership organization, it now has over 3,000 members, including companies, professionals, unions, government officials, academics, and interested individuals. It is funded entirely through the work it does. The staff includes persons with backgrounds in academia, law, and business.

The NCEO's mission is to provide the most objective, reliable information possible about employee ownership at the most affordable price possible. As part of the NCEO's commitment to providing objective information, it does not lobby or provide ongoing consulting services. The NCEO publishes a variety of materials on employee ownership and participation; it also holds approximately 50 workshops and conferences on employee ownership annually. The NCEO's work includes extensive contacts with the media, both through articles written for trade and professional publications and through interviews with reporters. The NCEO also maintains an extensive Web site at *www.nceo.org*. Finally, the NCEO has written or edited five books for outside publishers during the 1980s and 1990s.

Membership Benefits

NCEO members receive the following benefits:

- The bimonthly newsletter, *Employee Ownership Report,* which covers ESOPs, stock options, and employee participation.
- The *Employee Ownership Resource Guide,* which lists over 150 members who are employee ownership consultants.
- Substantial discounts on publications and events produced by the NCEO (such as this book).
- The right to telephone the NCEO for answers to general or specific questions regarding employee ownership.

An introductory NCEO membership costs $70 for one year ($80 outside North America) and covers an entire company at all locations, a single office of a firm offering professional services in this field, or an individual with a business interest in employee ownership. Full-time students and faculty members may join at the academic rate of $30 for one year ($40 outside North America).

Selected NCEO Publications on Employee Ownership and Participation

The NCEO offers a variety of publications on all aspects of employee ownership and participation, from employee stock ownership plans (ESOPs) to stock options to participative management. Following are descriptions of some of our main publications in these areas.

We publish new books and revise old ones on a yearly basis. To obtain the most current information on what we have available, visit our extensive Web site at *www.nceo.org* or call us at 510-208-1300.

Stock Options and Related Plans

- *The Stock Options Book* is a comprehensive resource covering the legal, tax, and design issues involved in implementing a stock option plan, especially a "broad-based" plan covering most or all employees. It is our main book on the subject.

Cost: $25 for NCEO members, $35 for nonmembers

- *Stock Options: Beyond the Basics* begins with a lengthy, comprehensive overview of stock options and related plans. The following chapters treat specialized topics such as repricing, securities issues, and evergreen options. The appendix is an exhaustive glossary of terms used in the field.

Cost: $25 for NCEO members, $35 for nonmembers

- *Model Equity Compensation Plans* provides examples of the plans discussed in the *Stock Options Book* (incentive stock option, nonqualified stock option, stock purchase, and phantom stock plans), together with brief explanations of the main documents. A disk is included with copies of the plan documents in formats any word processing program can open.

Cost: $50 for NCEO members, $75 for nonmembers

- *Current Practices in Stock Option Plan Design* is the full report on our 1998 survey of companies with broad-based stock option plans. It includes a detailed examination of plan design, use, and experience broken down by industry, size, and other categories. It has individual chapters on repricing; objectives, communications, and participation; and prior research in the field. An appendix discusses a 1999 survey we conducted.

Cost: $50 for NCEO members, $75 for nonmembers

- *An Overview of How Companies Are Granting Stock Options* is an executive summary of the survey results presented in *Current Practices in Stock Option Plan Design* (see above). *An Overview of How Companies Are Granting Stock Options* includes a sample (for the software industry) of the breakdowns by industry, region, and company size in *Current Practices*.

Cost: $10 for NCEO members, $15 for nonmembers; minimum order of 10 unless ordered with *Current Practices in Stock Option Plan Design*

- This book, *Incentive Compensation and Employee Ownership*, takes a broad look at how companies can use incentives, ranging from stock plans to cash bonuses to gainsharing, to motivate and reward employees. Includes both technical discussions and case studies.

  Cost: $25 for NCEO members, $35 for nonmembers

- *Equity-Based Compensation for Multinational Corporations* describes how companies can use stock options and other equity-based programs across the world to reward a global work force. It includes a country-by-country summary of tax and legal issues as well as a detailed case study.

  Cost: $25 for NCEO members, $35 for nonmembers

- *Communicating Stock Options* offers practical ideas and information about how to explain stock options to a broad group of employees. It includes the views of experienced practitioners as well as detailed examples of how companies communicate tax consequences, financial information, and other matters to employees.

  Cost: $35 for NCEO members, $50 for nonmembers

ESOPs

- *The ESOP Reader* is an overview of the issues involved in establishing and operating an ESOP. It covers the basics of ESOP rules, feasibility, valuation, and other matters, and then discusses managing an ESOP company, including brief case studies. The book is intended for publicly traded companies and anyone with a general interest in ESOPs and employee participation.

  Cost: $25 for NCEO members, $35 for nonmembers

- *Selling to an ESOP* is a guide for owners, managers, and advisors of closely held businesses. It explains how ESOPs work and then offers a comprehensive look at legal structures, valuation, financing (including self-financing), and other matters, especially the tax-deferred section 1042 "rollover" that allows owners to indefinitely defer capital gains taxation on the proceeds of the sale to the ESOP.

Cost: $25 for NCEO members, $35 for nonmembers

- *Leveraged ESOPs and Employee Buyouts* discusses how ESOPs borrow money to buy out entire companies, purchase shares from a retiring owner, or finance new capital. Beginning with a primer on leveraged ESOPs and their uses, it then discusses contribution limits, valuation, multi-investor buyouts, legal due diligence, transaction structures, accounting, feasibility studies, financing sources, and more. It is a useful companion to both *The ESOP Reader* and *Selling to an ESOP*.

  Cost: $25 for NCEO members, $35 for nonmembers

- The *Model ESOP* contains a sample ESOP plan, with alternative provisions given to tailor the plan to individual needs. It also includes a section-by-section explanation of the plan and other supporting materials.

  Cost: $50 for NCEO members, $75 for nonmembers

- The *Employee Ownership Q&A Disk* gives Microsoft Windows users (any version from Windows 3.1 onward) point-and-click access to 500 questions and answers on all aspects of ESOPs in a fully searchable hypertext format. The keyword search allows users to search the entire file in seconds and see all the search "hits" in context. Distributed on a 1.44 MB 3.5-inch diskette with a printed manual.

  Cost: $75 for NCEO members, $100 for nonmembers

- *An Introduction to ESOPs* is a 40-page booklet that explains how ESOPs work. Intended for readers who are deciding whether to implement an ESOP and also for relatively sophisticated ESOP participants who are interested in learning about the rules governing ESOPs.

  Cost: $1.75 for NCEO members, $2.50 for nonmembers; minimum order of 10 unless ordered with one of the ESOP publications listed above.

- The *ESOP Communications Sourcebook* is a looseleaf publication for ESOP companies. It includes ideas, reproducible forms, and examples on how to share financial information, explain ESOP features, and produce events to create an "ownership culture." It also addresses marketing employee ownership to customers.

  Cost: $35 for NCEO members, $50 for nonmembers

Employee Participation

- *Theory O: Creating an Ownership Style of Management* discusses how a company with an employee ownership plan can develop a better, more productive workplace through employee participation programs. Includes both a practical discussion of critical issues and 20 detailed case studies. Most of the companies that are discussed are ESOP companies, but a few use stock options.

  Cost: $20 for NCEO members, $30 for nonmembers

- *Open-Book Management and Corporate Performance* presents recent research on open-book management as well as case studies of companies that are implementing open-book management in a variety of ways.

  Cost: $20 for NCEO members, $30 for nonmembers

Also see *Communicating Stock Options to Employees* and the *ESOP Communications Sourcebook*, listed above.

Other

- *Section 401(k) Plans and Employee Ownership* focuses on how company stock is used in 401(k) plans, both in stand-alone 401(k) plans and combination 401(k)–ESOP plans ("KSOPs"). It addresses a whole range of issues that arise, including plan design, KSOPs, special techniques such as the "switchback," employee participation, and so on.

  Cost: $25 for NCEO members, $35 for nonmembers

- *The Journal of Employee Ownership Law and Finance* is the only professional journal solely devoted to employee ownership. Articles are written by leading experts and cover ESOPs, stock options, and related subjects in depth. The *Journal* appears four times a year and usually is from 140 to 200 pages long.

  Cost for one-year subscription:
  $75 for NCEO members, $100 for nonmembers

To join the NCEO as a member or to order any of the publications listed on the preceding pages, use the order form on the following page or use the secure ordering system on our Web site at *www.nceo.org*. If you join at the same time you order publications, you will receive the members-only publication discounts.

Order Form

To order, fill out this form and mail it with your credit card information or check to the NCEO at 1736 Franklin St., 8th Flr., Oakland, CA 94612; fax it with your credit card information to the NCEO at 510-272-9510; telephone us at 510-208-1300 with your credit card in hand; or order securely online at our Web site, *www.nceo.org*. If you are not already a member, you can join now to receive member discounts on the publications you order.

Name

Organization

Address

City, State, Zip (Country)

Telephone   Fax   E-mail

Method of Payment: ❑ Check (payable to "NCEO")   ❑ Visa   ❑ M/C   ❑ AMEX

Credit Card Number

Signature   Exp. Date

Title	Qty.	Price	Total

Tax: California residents add 8.25% sales tax (on publications only, not membership or Journal subscriptions)

Shipping: First publication $4, each additional $1 ($7 each outside North America); no shipping charges for membership or Journal subscriptions

Introductory NCEO Membership: $70 for one year ($80 outside North America)

Subtotal	$
Sales Tax	$
Shipping	$
Membership	$
TOTAL DUE	$